The Daily

GUID
INCOME
TAX

COMPLETELY UPDATED EDITION

PREPARED BY
David B. Genders, F.C.A.
A partner in Sayers Butterworth, Chartered Accountants

COLLINS
London and Glasgow

William Collins Sons & Co. Ltd.
London & Glasgow

First published 1974
Completely revised and reset edition 1977
Completely revised and reset edition 1978
Fully updated edition 1979
Completely revised and reset 1980
Fully updated edition 1981
Fully updated edition 1982
Fully updated edition 1983
Completely revised and reset 1984
Fully updated edition 1985
Fully updated edition 1986
Fully updated edition 1987
Fully updated edition 1988

© *Daily Telegraph* 1974, 1988
ISBN 0 00 434144 9
Printed in Great Britain

ACKNOWLEDGEMENT
The Inland Revenue forms reproduced in this book
are Crown copyright and are reproduced with the
permission of the Controller of Her Majesty's
Stationery Office.

CONTENTS

INTRODUCTION

'To tax and to please, no more than to love and be wise, is not given to men.'
— Edmund Burke

I feel sure this phrase echoes the sentiments of most of my readers. Nevertheless, while we may all harbour a dislike for taxation, we do have a responsibility for paying the taxes which are legally due from us. The purpose of this book is two-fold. Firstly, to help you understand your responsibilities as a taxpayer and deal with them in a proper manner. Secondly, while the book is not intended to be a comprehensive guide to every aspect of personal taxation, I hope it will also give you some ideas about how to reduce the amount of tax you pay each year.

This revised edition of the Guide incorporates the changes in legislation brought about by last year's Finance Acts. The major proposals on taxation announced by the Chancellor of the Exchequer in his 1988 Budget Statement are mentioned in the supplement at the end of the book.

1

HOW THE TAX SYSTEM WORKS

Before we look at the different types of taxable income and the various allowances and reliefs you can claim, I thought it would be helpful to give you an outline of the functions of the Inland Revenue departments which operate our tax system. Overall authority for administering the legislation enacted by Government is vested in the Board of Inland Revenue. Although there are now many specialist departments within the Inland Revenue it is likely that your only direct contact with the Revenue will be through your Inspector and Collector of Taxes.

The Inspector of Taxes

It is your Inspector of Taxes who sends out a Tax Return for you to complete every year. If you are either employed or a pensioner you can expect to receive this Return from the Inspector of Taxes who deals with the Pay-As-You-Earn affairs of your employer or his pension fund. It is not unusual for an employee's tax office to be many miles away from his home. For example, if you work in London your Inspector of Taxes is probably somewhere in Lancashire, Yorkshire or the West Country. Where you are self-employed you will find that your local tax office handles your Tax Returns.

Not only is your Inspector of Taxes responsible for sending you a Tax Return to complete but you can also expect to receive notices of coding, assessments and general correspondence on your affairs from the same office. A notice of coding tells you what allowances and reliefs are due to you, so indicating that part of your salary which is tax-free (see Chapter 4). An assessment is a calculation of the tax payable on a particular sort of income after deduction of any allowances or reliefs which are due to you.

The Collector of Taxes

The only responsibility of the Collector of Taxes, as the name implies, is to collect the tax which is due from you. Whenever your Inspector of Taxes sends an assessment to you the Collector is notified of the tax payable. If it is not paid by the due date you can expect to receive further demands until payment is made. Should you still fail to make payment the Collector will eventually institute proceedings for recovery of the tax by distraint.

If you are late in paying your tax and incur an interest charge it is the Collector who sends you a demand for the interest.

You can provide for the payment of a future tax liability by purchasing a Certificate of Tax Deposit. Certificates can be bought from the Collector of Taxes. They earn interest from the date of purchase up until the normal due date for payment of the liability (see Chapter 12). The interest is taxable.

Communicating with the Inland Revenue

On any straightforward matter where it helps you to have a quick answer it is better to telephone your tax office. Unless you specifically ask to speak to the Inspector you will be put through to one of his assistants who will usually be able to answer your enquiry. On a more involved aspect of your tax affairs I suggest you write to the tax office. Always remember to quote your reference number in any correspondence. Unfortunately, you may sometimes have difficulty in understanding the reply to your letter. I hope that by the time you have read this book you will be in a better position to decipher any correspondence, which at first sight looks horribly complicated. There are, of course, occasions when an exchange of letters will be initiated by your tax office. Where this happens, try to reply promptly and give the information requested in a clear and concise manner.

There may be times when a particular matter concerning your tax affairs can best be resolved by a detailed discussion. Then is the time to arrange a visit to your tax office. Where this is situated a long way from your place of employment or home you can always arrange to go to the nearest PAYE Enquiry Office. Remember that the Inspector of Taxes and his assistants are not responsible for making the legislation in our tax system. If you think you are being unfairly treated by the law there is no point in adopting an aggressive attitude at the interview. You will usually get a helpful response, especially if you adopt a polite approach to the Inspector or his assistant.

Where the Inspector has reason to believe that there has either been an omission of income from your Returns or an under-declaration of business profits he will often request a formal interview. At such a meeting the Inspector can be expected to pursue a wide-ranging line of questioning about your business activities and spending habits. You may well find some of the questions unreasonable or objectionable but it is one of the Inspector's duties to detect tax evasion and collect the tax due on the undeclared income. In the circumstances, the Inspector's line of questioning will probably be justified.

The Taxpayers' Charter
In 1986 the Inland Revenue brought together and published for the first time the principles which they try to meet in handling taxpayers' affairs. It is known as the Taxpayers' Charter and was published jointly with the H.M. Customs & Excise. It recognizes that taxpayers have important rights and are entitled to expect that:

Help and information

* The staff of the Inland Revenue and Customs and Excise will help you in every reasonable way to obtain your rights and to understand and meet your obligations under the tax laws. So that they can do this, the Inland Revenue and Customs and

Excise are entitled to expect that you will give them the full facts they need to decide how much tax you should pay.

Courtesy and consideration

* The staff of the Inland Revenue and Customs and Excise will at all times carry out their duties courteously, considerately and promptly.

Fairness

* You will have your tax liability decided impartially and be required to pay only the amount of tax properly due according to the law.

* You will be treated in the same way as other taxpayers in similar circumstances.

* You will be presumed to have dealt with your tax affairs honestly, unless there is reason to believe otherwise.

Privacy and confidentiality

* Information about your tax affairs which is supplied to the Inland Revenue or Customs and Excise will be treated in strict confidence and used only for purposes allowed by law.

Costs of compliance

* The Inland Revenue and Customs and Excise will have regard to the compliance costs of different taxpayers (including the particular circumstances of smaller businesses). In applying their procedures, they will recognize the need to keep to the minimum necessary the costs you incur in complying with the law, subject to their duty to collect the tax that is due from you efficiently and economically.

Independent appeal and review

* You may ask the Inland Revenue or Customs and Excise to look again at your case, if you think your tax bill is wrong or they have made a wrong decision, or they have handled your

tax affairs badly. Your case can be reviewed by the head of
the local office you are dealing with. If you are still not satisfied, you may take the matter up with the Inland Revenue
Regional Controller or the Collector of Customs and Excise,
or with their headquarters. Beyond that, you have important
rights to independent appeal.

* For Inland Revenue taxes, you may appeal against your tax
  bill to an independent tribunal, the appeal Commissioners,
  and if necessary to the courts.

* For Customs and Excise taxes and duties, you may appeal
  against a VAT decision to the independent VAT Tribunals; or
  in the case of other taxes or duties directly to the courts.

* You may ask your Member of Parliament to take up your case
  with the office you are dealing with, or with Treasury Minis-
  ters. Your Member of Parliament may also ask the independent Parliamentary Commissioner for Administration (the
  Ombudsman) to review your case, if you think that the
  Inland Revenue or Customs and Excise have handled your
  tax affairs improperly.

You can expect to receive a copy of the Charter along with
your tax return.

Changes in legislation

Every year, usually around Easter, the Chancellor of the
Exchequer makes his annual Budget Statement. Not only does
the Chancellor choose the occasion to introduce new or
amending legislation to our tax laws, but he also announces the
rates of tax and allowances for the following year.

The changes in legislation necessary to implement the
Chancellor's proposals are subsequently published in a
Finance Bill. The clauses in the Bill are debated and amend-
ments are proposed to some of them. Subsequently, the Bill is
passed by both Houses of Parliament and receives the Royal
Assent. It is then republished as a Finance Act.

It is the fiscal legislation passed by Parliament which is

administered by the Inland Revenue. On occasions when the law is either unclear or ambiguous the Inland Revenue publish a Statement of Practice showing how they intend to interpret it. There are also times when the Inland Revenue do not seek to apply the strict letter of the law. These are published as a list of Extra-Statutory Concessions.

The Inland Revenue also publish a number of booklets on different aspects of our tax system. A list of the most helpful booklets is set out in Table 1 at the end of the book.

Income Tax rates for 1987/88

Under our tax system, the tax (or fiscal) year runs from each 6 April to the following 5 April.

The rates of tax applying to all taxable income for 1987/8 are:

Band of Taxable Income £	Rate of Tax %	Tax on Band £	Cumulative Tax £
0—17,900	27	4,833	4,833
17,901—20,400	40	1,000	5,833
20,401—25,400	45	2,250	8,083
25,401—33,300	50	3,950	12,033
33,301—41,200	55	4,345	16,378
Over 41,200	60		

The law now provides that both the band of income taxable at the basic rate of 27% and the other rate bands are to be increased each tax year in line with the movement in the Retail Prices Index during the previous calendar year. As with the main personal allowances the Treasury can, however, order an increase different to the statutory commitment, providing Parliament agrees.

2

PERSONAL ALLOWANCES AND RELIEFS

The rates of the various personal allowances for 1987/88 are:

		£
Personal allowance	— single	2,425
	— married	3,795
Wife's earned income relief		2,425
Age allowance	— single (age 65-79)	2,960
	— married (age 65-79)	4,675
	— single (age 80 and over)	3,070
	— married (age 80 and over)	4,845
Additional personal allowance		1,370
Widow's bereavement allowance		1,370
Housekeeper relief		100
Son's or daughter's services		55
Dependent relative relief		100 or 145
Blind person's relief		540

There is a section in your Tax Return for you to claim the particular allowances to which you are entitled. They are deducted from your total income to give the amount on which you are liable to pay Income Tax each year.

It is usual for the rates of allowances to vary from year to year. This is particularly so now since the law provides that the rates of the allowances set out above, with the exception of the last four, are to go up at the beginning of each tax year in line with the increase in the Retail Prices Index during the previous calendar year. The Treasury can, however, order an increase different to the statutory commitment providing Parliament agrees. For 1987/88 the main personal tax allowances were raised by 3.7%. This was in line with the statutory requirement to compensate for inflation during 1986.

Personal allowances

If you are single, widowed, or your marriage has broken up you are entitled to the single personal allowance.

You will be due the higher married allowance if you are a married man whose wife is living with you. If you were married during the tax year the amount of your personal allowance depends upon when during the tax year the marriage took place. For every complete month from 6 April 1987 up to the date of your wedding the amount of your allowance is calculated by deducting from the value of the married allowance one twelfth of £1,370, that being the difference between the single and married allowances.

Illustration

A man who married on 16 July 1987 receives an allowance of £3,453 for 1987/88 as follows:

Married allowance	3,795
Less: Reduction	
3/12 × £1,370	342
1987/88 Allowance	£3,453

Wife's earned income relief

If you have a working wife she will benefit from being able to set this relief against her earnings. For this purpose earned income includes any pension she may be drawing from either the State or a previous employer's pension fund based on her own past contributions.

Age allowance

A pensioner whose income does not exceed a specified limit is entitled to a higher rate of personal allowance: this is known as the age allowance. It is due to a single person who is over age 65 during part or all of the tax year. For a married couple to benefit from this higher allowance it is only necessary for one of them to be at least 65 years old during part or all of the tax year. A single pensioner over 80 for part or all of the tax year receives a higher level of age allowance. The same goes for a married couple, although only one of them need be at least 80 years old.

As the age allowance is designed to help those pensioners who are less well off, it reduces where their income rises above £9,800 for 1987/88. The reduction in the age allowance is two thirds of the amount by which total income exceeds the stated limit of £9,800, although it cannot take the rate of the allowance below the level of either the single or married allowance as the case may be. It follows that no measure of age allowance is due to an elderly couple (age 65-79) whose joint income exceeds £11,120 for 1987/88. For a single pensioner (age 65-79) this limit is £10,602. For a married couple or a single person aged 80 or over, these same income limits are £11,375 and £10,767 respectively.

Illustration
An elderly married couple in their late 60s whose joint income amounted to £10,400 during 1987/88 are entitled to an allowance of £4,275, as follows:

	£
Income before tax	
State pension	3,289
Pension from former employer	4,700
Investment income	2,411
	10,400
Less: Income limit for age allowance	9,800
Excess	£600
Age allowance	4,675
Less: Reduction — 2/3 × 600	400
1987/88 Allowance	£4,275

The income limit for age allowance goes up each tax year in the same way as the main personal allowances.

Additional personal allowance
To qualify for this allowance you must be a person, such as a widow, widower or divorcee, who is not entitled to claim the married allowance, or a married man whose wife is either

physically incapacitated or mentally infirm. In either event you must have at least one child living with you who fulfils certain conditions. If the child is your own he or she must be under 16 at the start of the tax year. If older, he or she must still be at school or attending a full-time course at a university, college or similar place of education, including a training course for at least two years with an employer in some trade or profession. Where the child living with you is not your own then he or she must be under 18 years old at the beginning of the tax year and looked after at your own expense.

No matter how many children you may have living with you who fulfil these tests only one allowance can be claimed. If more than one person is in a position to claim the allowance for the same child then it will be apportioned between them.

Widow's bereavement allowance

Providing her husband was entitled to the married man's allowance at the time of his death, a widow can claim this allowance for both the tax year in which her husband dies and the following tax year as long as she has not remarried by the beginning of that year. As a wife who loses her husband during a tax year then becomes taxable as a single person, the bereavement allowance for that year is given as a deduction against her income from that moment onwards until the end of the tax year. For the following tax year this allowance is set against her total income.

Housekeeper relief

A widow or widower can claim this relief if he or she has a relative or a paid help living in as a housekeeper. If the housekeeper is a relative who is married, the opportunity for claiming this allowance is lost where the relative or her husband is receiving the married allowance. Furthermore, the housekeeper relief cannot be claimed if you are claiming the additional personal allowance.

Son's or daughter's services

A person who is elderly or sick enough to be forced to depend upon the services of a son or daughter can claim this relief. The son or daughter must live in and be supported by the claimant.

Dependent relative relief

This is an allowance for a person who helps towards supporting his own or his wife's dependent relative. The relative must be either a pensioner or too unwell to look after himself or herself, unless the relative is the claimant's mother or mother-in-law when it is sufficient if she is either widowed, separated or divorced. The higher allowance of £145 is given to a woman not living with her husband for each dependent relative for whom she can claim.

Where two or more people are in a position to claim for the same relative the allowance is apportioned between them. If the dependent relative's income exceeds the amount of the basic National Insurance Pension for a tax year the rate of allowance is reduced by the amount of the excess. The effect of this restriction is often to remove the ability to make a claim for this relief.

Blind person's relief

This relief is given to a registered blind person. If both husband and wife are blind they may each claim the relief. A blind person who could also claim the relief for the services of a son or daughter should forego that allowance as otherwise the blind person's relief will not be given.

Relief on life assurance premiums

These days life assurance serves many purposes. They range from providing for the payment of lump sums on death to either pay off the amount of an outstanding mortgage or leave a lump sum for the deceased's dependents, to other uses which can often serve as tax-efficient forms of investment.

The amount of tax relief on life assurance premiums is at the fixed rate of 15% on policies taken out before 14 March 1984. It should not be necessary for you to claim this since the premiums paid to the life assurance company are after deduction of the 15% tax relief. There are occasions when some or all of this relief can be withdrawn, and then a payment to the Inland Revenue will have to be made for the tax relief which has been lost. For example, the amount of premiums which can be paid in any tax year without restriction of the tax relief is limited to £1,500 or one sixth of your total income, before allowances, whichever is greater.

Illustration
A couple pay annual life assurance premiums of £1,700 before tax relief. If their income is:
  (a) £12,000, the 15% tax relief is unrestricted;
  (b) £8,000, they will only receive the 15% tax relief on premiums of £1,500.

Premiums payable on a life assurance policy taken out after 13 March 1984 do not attract any tax relief. The same applies to future premiums payable on a policy taken out before that date if, after 13 March 1984, the benefits secured under the policy are varied or its terms extended.

3

INTEREST PAYMENTS AND OTHER OUTGOINGS

As the opportunities to claim tax relief for interest paid on borrowed money are limited, you should be aware of the few occasions when you can do so. It is important to appreciate that the purpose for which a loan is raised governs whether the interest on it will be eligible for tax relief. How the loan is secured is irrelevant.

Generally the interest on which tax relief is due is deducted from your total income in the year of payment. This general rule does not apply where you borrow money to buy a property which you let out: this is dealt with later on in the chapter.

Your own home
If you have borrowed money from a building society, a bank or some other source to help you buy your home you will receive tax relief on the interest you pay each year. Your home can be a house or a flat; it may even be a houseboat or a caravan. For this purpose a caravan must be at least 22 ft long and 7 ft 6 in wide or permanently situated so that it is liable to local authority rates.

It is not only the purchase price of your home which governs the maximum amount of the loan on which interest qualifies for tax relief. The incidental costs of buying your home such as surveyor's and solicitor's fees and stamp duty all count as part of the cost price.

From time to time you may improve your home by perhaps either extending it or installing double glazing. If you meet this type of expenditure by either increasing your mortgage or taking a loan from your bank the interest will qualify for tax relief. The Inland Revenue has issued a list of most, but not all, of the types of expenditure on property improvements qualifying for tax relief. On the list are:

(1) Home extensions and loft conversions.
(2) Central and solar heating installations (excluding portable radiators and night storage radiators not fixed to a permanent spur outlet). The cost of replacing one form of heating with another (for example changing from oil to gas central heating) is included.
(3) Installation of double-glazing even though it is in a detachable form. Replacement of windows or doors generally is included.
(4) Insulation of roof or walls.
(5) Installation of bathrooms and other similar plumbing.
(6) Kitchen and bedroom units (for example sink units) which are affixed to and become part of the building. In practice a range of matching units may be treated as qualifying as a whole even though only some of them qualify (but always excluding cookers, refrigerators and similar appliances).
(7) Connection to main drainage.
(8) Erection and cost of garages, garden sheds, greenhouses, patios and fences.
(9) Recovering or reconstructing a roof.
(10) Construction or landscaping of gardens.
(11) Construction of swimming pools.
(12) Reconstruction of property, e.g. conversion into flats.
(13) Underpinning a house.
(14) Rebuilding a facade.
(15) Insertion or renewal of damp-proof course. Dry and wet-rot treatment.
(16) Replacement of electrical installations.
(17) Extensive repointing, pebble-dashing, texture coating or stone cladding (but excluding painting).
(18) Installation of fire or burglar alarms.
(19) Installation of water-softening equipment forming a permanent part of the plumbing system.
(20) Construction of driveways and paths.
(21) Extensive replacement of guttering.

There is an overall limit on the amount of your loans for the purchase and improvement of your home above which the interest is no longer deductible from your income: for 1987/88 this limit is £30,000.

Illustration

Year	Expenditure		Amount Borrowed	Interest Paid
1978	House purchase	40,000		
	Professional fees and stamp duty	1,600		
		£41,600	£24,000 at 11% p.a.	2,640
1980	Double glazing installed	£3,000	£2,500 at 15% p.a.	375
1982	House extended	£8,000	£6,000 at 13% p.a.	780

Since the 1982 loan of £6,000 took the total borrowings above £30,000, not all the interest paid in 1987/88 on this latest loan will qualify for tax relief:

Interest paid: on 1978 and 1980 loans of £26,500	3,015
on 1982 loan: $\dfrac{3,500}{6,000} \times £780$	455
1987/88 Relief for interest paid	£3,470

If you are employed in some capacity that requires you to live in accommodation provided by your employer you can still in certain specific circumstances obtain mortgage interest relief on a loan to buy your own home. This also applies if you are self-employed and the terms of your trade or profession are such that you must live in accommodation provided for your use.

Most people move home at some time during their lifetime. It is often impossible to arrange for the sale of your present home to coincide with the purchase of your new one. To overcome such difficulties it is usual to arrange a short-term bridging loan. For a period up to one year (or longer, at the Inland Revenue's discretion), interest payable on both the existing mortgage and the bridging loan will both qualify for tax relief, subject of course to the overall limitation of £30,000 on each loan.

Most of you are making your regular mortgage repayments after deduction of tax at the basic rate on the interest element in each repayment. This procedure is known as 'Mortgage Interest Relief at Source' — MIRAS for short. You do not have to pay this tax over to the Inland Revenue. This applies even where you have no taxable income, or where your income is less than your personal allowances. If your mortgage exceeds the limitation of £30,000 on which interest qualifies for tax relief you will receive relief on that part of the total interest payable equivalent to this limit. This relief is obtained either through the new tax deduction scheme or, as previously, through your PAYE coding. Only tax at the basic rate is taken off the interest at the time of payment, but despite that you are not denied relief at the higher rates of tax. This will still be given to you where your top rate of Income Tax is in excess of the basic rate.

A second home

If you can afford to run two homes — such as a house or flat in town for use during the weekdays and a cottage in the country for weekends — you will nevertheless only be able to claim tax relief on a loan to buy one of them. This will be granted on the mortgage interest to buy whichever of your homes is the main one. You cannot decide this for yourself. It is a matter of fact.

Alternatively, you may want to provide a flat or cottage for an elderly relative to live in. If you borrow money to help purchase a suitable home the interest on the loan will qualify for tax relief as long as the total amount of any borrowing for this purpose together with any outstanding mortgage on your own home does not exceed the overall limitation of £30,000. Where the amount of an additional loan lifts your borrowings above this threshold the interest on which tax relief will be given is proportionally reduced as already illustrated in this chapter.

The relative must be either a pensioner or too unwell to look after himself or herself, unless the relative is the claimant's mother or mother-in-law, when it is sufficient if she is either widowed, separated or divorced.

Let property

Interest on a loan taken out to buy or improve a property which you rent out is tax deductible. The interest is set against the rental income from the property. Should the interest payable in a tax year exceed the rents receivable in the same year, the excess can only be carried forward to future years.

Illustration

A property was bought in 1981 with the assistance of a £35,000 loan. It is let and the rents less expenses came to £4,000 and £6,000 during 1986/87 and 1987/88 respectively.

	1986/87 £		1987/88 £
Rents less expenses	4,000		6,000
Less: Loan interest paid	4,900	4,200	
Deficit carried forward	£900	900	
			5,100
1987/88 Taxable Income			£900

The property must be let at a commercial rent for at least 26 weeks in any period of 52 weeks. When it is not let it must either be available for letting or be undergoing repairs or renovations.

Business loans

Most businesses need to borrow money at some time for one purpose or another. Interest on any such borrowings is allowable as a deduction against your business profits providing the borrowed money is used for business purposes. It does not matter for this purpose whether the borrowings arise because your bank account goes overdrawn, or because you take out a loan for some specific purpose connected with your business.

If you need to borrow to buy an asset — such as a car or a piece of machinery — for use in your business, the interest you pay will qualify for tax relief but will be restricted where the asset is also used privately.

If you are about to become a member of a partnership, you

may need to borrow money to purchase a share in the partnership or to contribute capital for use in its business. If that is the case, the interest on the borrowings will qualify for tax relief.

Alternatively, you may have business connections with a private company. The interest on a loan raised so you can either acquire shares in the company or lend it money for use in its business will qualify for tax relief. You must either own at least 5% of the company's share capital or have at least some shareholding and work for the greater part of your time in the business.

Employees who need to borrow to buy shares in their company as part of an employee buy-out are allowed tax relief on the interest.

Replacement loans

There are occasions when you might want to take out a fresh loan in order to repay an existing borrowing. If the interest on the mortgage or loan which is being replaced qualifies for tax relief then the interest on the replacement loan will also qualify for tax relief in the same way.

Deeds of covenant

Later on in this book (Chapter 8) we shall see how useful deeds of covenant can be when they are taken out in favour of children. They are also an effective way of making a donation to a charity. To be valid for tax purposes a deed must be capable of providing for regular annual payments over a minimum period of seven years, except where it is for the benefit of a charity. Then it is sufficient if a deed can exceed a period of only three years. The payer must deduct Income Tax at the basic rate from every payment under a deed. The tax deducted can be retained providing the payer has suffered tax at the basic rate which is at least equivalent to the tax deducted from all covenanted payments during a tax year.

It is the ability of the recipient to recover the Income Tax deducted which will often persuade the payer to take out a deed of covenant. This will always apply where charities are involved as they are exempt from tax on their income. As an incentive to individuals with high incomes they are allowed to deduct covenanted payments to charities from their income in calculating their higher-rate tax liabilities.

Alimony and maintenance payments

Where a marriage breaks down the husband will usually have to make payments to his former or separated wife under either a court order or a separation agreement. Income Tax at the basic rate must be deducted from these payments. Sometimes a court order can require that payements be made to the couple's children for their education and maintenance. These should also be made under deduction of tax unless they qualify as small maintenance payments. This is dealt with more fully in Chapter 7.

4

EARNINGS FROM EMPLOYMENT

Most of you will be familiar with at least some part or other of
the Pay As You Earn (PAYE) system. It provides a mechanism
for collecting the tax due on the earnings of those people in
employment. Employers must deduct Income Tax from the
earnings of their employees and every month the total of these
deductions has to be paid over to the Inland Revenue. The
PAYE taken off an employee's earnings is treated as a credit
against the overall amount of tax payable by the employee for
the tax year in question. In working out the amount of tax to
deduct from each employee's salary or pay packet, the
employer takes into account each individual's own allowances
and other reliefs. This is possible because the Inland Revenue
issue employers with a code number for each employee. In
turn the code number incorporates each employee's allowances and reliefs. The system allows for these to be spread
evenly throughout the tax year to avoid any substantial varia-
tion in the amount of tax deducted from each salary cheque or
pay packet.

The sort of earnings which count as taxable income from an
employment are:

> An annual salary or wage
> Overtime
> Commission
> Tips or gratuities
> Holiday pay
> Sick pay
> Earnings from a part-time employment
> Directors' fees or other remuneration
> Benefits-in-kind

Code numbers

I have already mentioned that each employee is issued with a
code number by the tax office. In theory the code number
should ensure that the correct amount of tax has been
deducted from your earnings by the end of the tax year. The
system can only work properly and effectively if your local tax
office is kept informed of any changes in your personal circumstances which affect the amount of your allowances or reliefs.
For example, most if not all notices of coding for the 1988/89 tax
year commencing on 6 April 1988 were issued during the early
part of the year. This was before people came to complete their
1988/89 Income Tax Returns. The Return requires a report of
each person's income for the tax year just finished — the year to
5 April 1988 — but the claim for allowances is for the following
year — the year to 5 April 1989. It follows that the information
on which all the code numbers for 1988/89 have been based is
that of the previous year. This is why it is important you should
check your code number for 1988/89 and write to your tax office
setting out any alterations that are required to your allowances
or reliefs. If the rate of any allowance has been altered in the
Budget there is no need for you to communicate with your tax
office — your employer will automatically have been instructed
by the Inland Revenue about how to deal with this.

On the following page is an illustration of a notice of coding
for 1988/89. It shows the taxpayer is a married man claiming
relief for a dependent relative. His personal allowances for
1988/89 are £3,895 before deductions. The first three of these
relate to benefits-in-kind in the form of a company car and
private medical insurance cover provided by the taxpayer's
employer. Some of the types of taxable expenses and benefits
are dealt with later on in the chapter. The coding notice illus-
trates how the tax payable on benefits-in-kind is usually collected. This is done by restricting the taxpayer's allowances by
the value of the benefits-in-kind. In the illustration they come
to £1,570 reducing the allowances to £2,325. The final deduction is for tax underpaid for 1986/87 of £84. For any one of a
number of reasons the allowances given in the coding notice
may subsequently turn out to differ from those actually due to
the taxpayer. If, as a result, there is an underpayment of tax this

SPECIMEN FORM

Inland Revenue
PAYE-Notice of coding
Please keep this notice for future
reference and let me know of any
change in your address. The enclosed
notes explain the entries.

Issued by
H.M. Inspector of Taxes
Fieldgate District,
Fieldgate House,
Fieldgate, TA6 7DP

Mr. D. Jones,
79 Acorn Street,
Fieldgate,
TA6 2RY

Please use this reference if you write or
call. It will help to avoid delay.

195/F249				
FX	57	30	29	C

Date

This notice cancels any previous notice of coding for the year shown below. It shows the allowances which make up your code.
Your employer or paying officer will use this code to deduct or refund the right amount of tax under PAYE during the year shown
below.
Please check this notice. If you think it is wrong please return it to me and give your reasons. If we cannot agree you have the right
of appeal.
Please let me know at once about any change in your personal circumstances which may alter your allowances and coding.

See Note	Allowances	£	See Note	Less Deductions	£
17	Personal	3,795	25	Medical Insurance	200
17	Dependent Relative	100	25	Benefits (Car)	770
			25	Benefits (Car Fuel)	600
			29	Unpaid Tax £84.00	311
				Less total deductions	1881
	Total allowances	3,895		Allowances set against pay etc. £	2014

Your code for the year to 5 April 1989   **is**   201H   **Please see Part overleaf**

P2 (T)

is often collected in a later year, again by restricting the allowances in the coding. In our illustration a reduction in allowances for 1988/89 of £311 will result in the Inland Revenue collecting the underpayment of £84 (£311 at 27%) from the taxpayer during the year.

The combined effect of these adjustments is to leave the taxpayer with allowances of only £2,014 to be set against his salary for 1988/89. His code number will be 201H. Clearly, there is a direct link between the taxpayer's allowances and his code number. The suffix letter is added to the coding so that whenever there is a change in the rates of personal allowances it can be automatically implemented by the employer. The letter H indicates the taxpayer is entitled to the married man's personal allowance. A coding which includes the single personal allowance or the wife's earned income relief ends up with the letter L. For personal reasons you may not want your employer to know which personal allowance you are claiming. You should then ask for the suffix letter T to be included in your coding. Your employer must then wait for instructions from the tax office before making any changes to the coding. Where you have more than one employment you will probably find that all your allowances are given in calculating the PAYE due from your main employment. Your earnings from a subsidiary employment are likely to attract a coding prefixed by either the letter D or BR. A 'D' coding results in tax being deducted at one of the higher rates whereas 'BR' instructs the employer to deduct tax at the basic rate.

The assessment
Shortly after the end of each tax year every employer sends in to the Inland Revenue a Return summarizing the names of all employees, their earnings during the tax year, and the Income Tax deducted from them. At the same time the employer hands out a Form P60 to every employee. This is a certificate of the employee's earnings for the past tax year and the Income Tax deducted from them. For most employees this corresponds with the tax due on their earnings. It is not then necessary for the Inland Revenue to issue an assessment. You can, however, always ask for one.

If you do receive an assessment it will show the earnings from all your employments during the past tax year together with the amounts of tax deducted by your employers. If you were provided with any benefits-in-kind, such as the use of a company car, the value of these will be shown on the assessment as an addition to your salary or wages. This information is supplied to your tax office by your employer on a Form P11D. The types of benefit-in-kind which are taxable are dealt with later on in this chapter. In addition to detailing your earnings, the assessment will also show the allowances and reliefs you have been given. The final part is a calculation of the Income Tax due for the year. The tax deducted by your employer under PAYE is set against the liability to arrive at the overall position. An assessment which shows an overpayment is always a welcome sight. It will usually come to you with a cheque in repayment of the tax overpaid. Alternatively, the Inspector of Taxes might ask you to complete a formal claim to repayment before the Inland Revenue send you their cheque. If you have not paid enough tax you may be asked to send the Inland Revenue a cheque for the underpayment. Where it is not substantial the Inspector of Taxes will usually decide to collect it by restricting your allowances through an amendment to your notice of coding. We have already seen how this works. You should check the assessment as soon as possible after you receive it. If you want to dispute the income on which your tax has been calculated the Inland Revenue allow you only thirty days to write about this.

Expenses

The rules which allow you to claim tax relief on expenses relating to an employment are extremely restrictive. They dismiss the possibility of claiming tax relief on almost all types of expenses which are not ultimately borne by the employer. This is because the employee has to show that any expenditure is incurred 'wholly, exclusively and necessarily' while performing the duties of the employment. If the employer has not been prepared to foot the bill for the expenditure involved, then the Inland Revenue infer it was incurred more as a matter of choice than of necessity. Nevertheless, where you personally meet

Tax saver

the cost of an annual subscription to a professional body, you should include details on your Tax Return as it is deductible from your income. The Inland Revenue and the Trade Unions have agreed flat rate allowances for the upkeep of tools and special clothing for most classes of industry. The rates for 1986/87 are set out in Table 3. As an alternative, the individual may claim a deduction for his actual expenses on these items.

Most expenses you incur in your job or employment are probably borne by your employer, who either reimburses you on an expense claim or pays for them direct. Employees (including full-time working directors who own 5% or under of the company's shares) earning less than £8,500 per annum including expenses are not taxed on most benefits or perks provided by their employers. Other directors and employees (including full-time working directors), whose total earnings, including expenses, exceed £8,500 per annum, are generally taxed on the actual value of any benefits obtained from their employments. If you fall within this category we have already seen that information about your expense payments and benefits-in-kind is supplied to your tax office annually on a Form P11D. It is down to you to justify that you are not to be taxed on them. This should not cause you any difficulties where the expenses, such as travelling and entertaining, have genuinely arisen during the performance of the duties of your employment.

Luncheon Vouchers up to 15p per day are tax free for everyone, but remember that the cost of travelling between your home and the office is not allowable for tax purposes. The only exception to this rule is the cost of infrequent public transport met by your employer when you have been working late, and public transport is either no longer available or it would be unreasonable to expect you to use it at a late hour. Infrequent late working means a requirement to work until at least 9.00 p.m. not more than 60 times in a tax year.

The value of some benefits provided for directors or higher-paid employees are, however, calculated differently.

(a) Company cars
Generally regarded as the most valuable benefit which can be provided to a director or higher-paid employee, it is measured

according to a fixed scale. For cars with an original value up to £19,250 this is determined by their cubic capacity. For more luxurious cars the benefit is governed by price alone. The full scale of benefits is:

Original Market Value of Company Car	1987/88		1988/89	
	Under 4 years old	4 or more years old	Under 4 years old	4 or more years old
	£	£	£	£
Up to £19,250				
1400 c.c. or less	525	350	580	380
1401 c.c. to 2000 c.c.	700	470	770	520
Over 2000 c.c.	1,100	725	1,210	800
£19,251 to £29,000	1,450	970	1,595	1,070
Over £29,000	2,300	1,530	2,530	1,635

Where the business usage in a tax year is more than 18,000 miles the scale benefit is halved. Where it is under 2,500 miles per annum it is increased to $1\frac{1}{2}$ times the amounts in the above table. Mileage between your home and place of business counts as private, not business, usage. The $1\frac{1}{2}$-times rate is also charged where a director or higher-paid employee has a second company car.

If it is the company's policy to meet the cost of petrol for private motoring there is an additional taxable benefit. Again it is based on predetermined fixed amounts dependent on the cubic capacity of the company car, as follow:

Cubic Capacity	1987/88 and 1988/89
	£
1400 c.c. or less	480
1401 c.c. to 2000 c.c.	600
Over 2000 c.c.	900

(b) Living accommodation
In some trades it is established practice for the employer to

provide living accommodation. This can also be desirable where there is a security risk. In either sort of situation no tax liability will fall on the director or higher-paid employee.

In other circumstances the director or higher-paid employee is chargeable to Income Tax on the annual value of the property after deducting any rent paid for it. The annual value of a property for these purposes is broadly equivalent to the gross rateable value. The director or higher-paid employee faces an additional tax charge where the accommodation costs more than £75,000.

(c) Beneficial loans

Loans from an employer which are either interest free or where the interest charged by the employer is below a commercial rate can give rise to a taxable benefit on the director or higher-paid employee. The benefit is calculated by applying the Inland Revenue's official rate of interest to the loan. At present the official rate is 10.5% per annum. The benefit is reduced by any interest actually paid on the loan. No charge to tax arises where the value of the benefit is less than £200, or where the loan is for a purpose on which the interest would qualify for tax relief (see Chapter 3).

Share options

No liability to Income Tax is imposed on a director or employee who acquires or disposes of ordinary shares under his employer's Approved Share Option Scheme. An option must be exercised not less than three, or more than ten, years after it is granted, nor under three years after a previous exercise. The gain is measured by the difference between the sale proceeds and the cost of acquiring the shares, and is charged to Capital Gains Tax at the time of disposal. The price payable under the option agreement must not be less than the market value of the shares at the date the option is granted.

A number of other requirements must be met by both the employee and the employing company. These are, however, less onerous than those in earlier profit-sharing and savings-related schemes.

Donations to charity

You can make donations to charity by way of regular deduc- **Tax**
tions from your salary by your employer, if your employer **save**
operates such a scheme through an approved agency charity.
Employers are not bound to launch schemes and employees
can choose whether to participate in them. If you do so, you
will be entitled to tax relief on donations not exceeding £120
annually.

Working abroad

Where your job takes you overseas for long periods of absence
then your tax treatment in the U.K. is worked out on a favourable basis. Providing you can establish a consecutive period of
at least 365 days working overseas the exemption from Income
Tax on the earnings from that employment is 100%. You are
allowed intermittent visits to the U.K. in establishing a qualifying period of at least 365 days. These must not amount to more
than 62 days, nor in building up the qualifying period must
they come to more than one sixth of the period starting from
the outset. If you work abroad for a complete tax year you will
probably become non-resident. This is dealt with more fully in
Chapter 9.

Tax relief is allowed on travel expenses you incur in relation
to your overseas employment. Nor will you be taxed on the
cost of board and lodging provided for you where the expenses
are borne by your employer.

Generally, whenever your job takes you overseas, even
for short periods, you will not be taxed on the cost of your
travelling expenses so long as your employer meets the bills.
This also applies to the costs of unlimited return visits to the
U.K. during longer assignments abroad.

No taxable benefit arises where your employer meets the
travelling costs of your wife and children to visit you overseas.
Not more than two return visits by the same person are
allowed each year, and you must be working abroad for a con-
tinuous period of at least 60 days.

Payments on termination of employment

It is now common practice for an employee to be paid a lump
sum on the termination of an employment. If the right to
receive the payment arose during the period of employment
then it is taxable in full in the same way as other earnings.
Otherwise the lump sum payment is either wholly or partly tax
free. The occasions when the payments are free of tax are:

(1) Where the employment ceases because of the death,
    injury or disability of the employee.

(2) Where most of the employee's time was spent working
    overseas for the employer.

(3) Where the lump sum payment is under £25,000.

Where the amount of the lump sum payment is more than
£25,000 only the part of it over this limit is taxable. Nevertheless, the tax due is reduced. By how much the tax is reduced
depends on the size of the lump sum payment. The taxable
amount is treated as your top slice of income and the Income
Tax payable on it is worked out. The reduction in tax payable is
calculated according to the following table:

Slice of Lump Sum Payment	Relief from Tax
First £25,000	Exempt
Next £25,000	Tax reduced by one half
Next £25,000	Tax reduced by one quarter
Excess over £75,000	Taxed in full

Illustration
An employee who lost his job last September was paid a lump sum of
£40,000 on the termination of his employment. He is a married man and his
earnings during 1987/88 were £20,000. The couple's investment income
was £3,500 for the same year. The taxable part of the lump sum is £15,000.

	Tax Payable	
	Ignoring lump sum	With lump sum
	£	£
Income		
Earnings	20,000	20,000
Taxable part of lump sum	—	15,000
Investment income	3,500	3,500
	23,500	38,500
Less: Personal allowance	3,795	3,795
	£19,705	£34,705
Income tax thereon:		
First 17,900 at 27%	4,833.00	4,833.00
Next 1,805/2,500 at 40%	722.00	1,000.00
Next 5,000 at 45%	—	2,250.00
Next 7,900 at 50%	—	3,950.00
Next 1,405 at 55%	—	772.75
	£5,555.00	£12,805.75

Tax due on lump sum:
$\frac{1}{2} \times$ (£12,805.75 − £5,555.00) = £3,625.37

As your employer will operate PAYE on the taxable amount of the lump sum payment you will probably be due a refund as it is likely that too much tax will be deducted.

Any statutory redundancy payment you receive, although exempt from tax itself, has to be counted in with any other lump sum payment from your employer in working out the tax due on the lump sum.

National Insurance
Although it is not within the scope of this book to go into National Insurance in detail I cannot pass on to the next chapter without mentioning it briefly. During recent years it has had an ever increasing impact on your salary cheque or pay

packet. Although certain allowances and reliefs are deductible in calculating how much Income Tax you pay on your earnings, no similar rules apply for National Insurance purposes. The rate of contribution is applied to your gross earnings. The rates and the earnings levels on which they are calculated are set out in Table 3 at the end of the book.

5

THE SELF-EMPLOYED

You cannot simply choose to be taxed on your earnings as a self-employed person. It is a matter of fact whether you are working on your own account or for someone else as an employee. You are *not* self-employed if your are running your business through a company. If you are employed but have some other freelance business activity as well, you will be taxed on these profits as a self-employed person.

The obligations imposed on the taxpayer who is self-employed are more onerous than those which apply to the employee. Proper records must be maintained of all business transactions. At the end of each financial year they are all brought together into an account of the income and expenditure of the business for the past twelve months. Whenever possible a balance sheet should be drawn up showing the assets and liabilities of the business at the year end. It is also better to operate your business through a separate bank account.

Value Added Tax
Unless the turnover of your business is under £21,300 per annum it must be registered with the Customs and Excise for the purposes of Value Added Tax. If your takings are not up to this level you will only need to register when they amount to more than £7,250 in the previous calendar quarter, unless you can demonstrate your total turnover for the year will still not exceed £21,300. Even if your turnover at the end of a 12 month period exceeds the registration limit, you will not have to register providing the Customs and Excise are satisfied that your business takings will not exceed £21,300 over the next year.

If you are liable to register, Customs and Excise must be notified not later than 30 days after the end of the appropriate calendar quarter. Failure to do so will lead to the imposition of a penalty. It amounts to £50 where no tax is due, or the greater of £50 and 30% of the tax due for the period beginning on the date when registration was required and ending when your application for registration is received or liability to be registered is discovered. The imposition of a penalty can be avoided where you can demonstrate there was a reasonable excuse for your conduct. However, apart from very exceptional circumstances, such an appeal is unlikely to be successful.

If you have been registered for at least two years but your turnover is falling you may want to apply to have your registration cancelled. You can do this providing the Customs and Excise are satisfied that your predictable future turnover will not exceed £20,300, inclusive of VAT, in any 12 month period.

When you need to register you should ask for Form VAT 1 — 'Value Added Tax — Application for Registration' — from your local Customs and Excise office. Soon after you have completed the form and sent it off you will receive your registration certificate and a selection of notices and leaflets. These are intended both to help you to understand the workings of the tax, and to assist you in complying with all the rules and regulations.

As a registered business you are required to charge VAT on all your taxable supplies. There are two rates: nil, and the standard rate of 15%. Some types of business, for example those relating to finance and education, are exempt from VAT. The turnover from these does not count towards the £21,300 registration limit, and VAT on expenditure incurred in these activities cannot be recovered.

Every three months you have to complete a Return — Form VAT 100 — of all the VAT charged on your supplies or services during the period. From this total is deducted the VAT you have incurred on business purchases and overhead expenses for the same period. Where the Return ends up showing an amount due to the Customs and Excise you should send it off with a cheque in settlement of the amount due. If the VAT suffered on your business expenditure exceeds the VAT charged on your sales, the Return will show you are entitled to a repayment. This will be sent to you by the Customs and Excise.

A business with a taxable turnover of up to £250,000 per annum can now apply to account for VAT on the straightforward basis of cash receipts and payments.

Over the years many businesses have adopted an indifferent attitude in their approach to the completion of Returns and the payment of VAT. As a direct result the Government introduced the Default Surcharge, which came into operation in 1986. Under these rules your business will be in default if its VAT Returns and the tax due on it do not reach the Customs and Excise by the due date. This is normally one month after the end of the period covered by the Return. If your business fails to meet the deadline twice in any 12-month period, it will receive an envelope containing a Surcharge Liability Notice. This will warn you that the business will have to pay a surcharge on any VAT involved if it defaults once more in the following 12 months. The surcharge is a percentage of the VAT due for the period covered by the late Return. It starts at 5% of the VAT owed by your business, and increases on each subsequent occasion the business defaults up to a maximum of 30% of the VAT due.

Every now and then a Customs and Excise officer will visit you to make sure that you are keeping proper records of your business transactions and correctly dealing with your quarterly Returns. You should keep all your invoices as evidence of the VAT suffered on purchases and other expenses.

If you are in the retail trade there are special schemes for calculating how much VAT you need to pay. There are also particular rules which apply to items such as second-hand goods, motor cars (including fuel provided for private motoring) and business entertainment. It is outside the scope of this book to go into these and others in detail.

Accounts
You can choose the date to which you make up the accounts of your trade or business each year. For this reason it is unlikely that the first accounts will cover a full year's trading activities. Thereafter your accounts should continue to be made up to the

same date every year although you can alter this where you can show good reason for a change.

Your accounts should be drawn up to show the profit or loss earned in the financial year. This is not usually the simple difference between the cash received and the cash paid out. For example, if you sell to some of your customers on credit there will inevitably be some unpaid invoices at the end of the financial year. Nevertheless, the amount of these outstanding invoices needs to come into your accounts as income for that period. Equally, where amounts are owing to your suppliers at the year-end these must be brought into the accounts as expenses incurred in the year. If your trade is one where you need to keep a stock of raw materials or finished goods, the value of that stock at the year-end must enter your accounts. It will usually be valued at cost or, in the case of redundant or old stock, at realizable value.

Tax saver Make sure you include in your accounts all the expenses of running your business. If, for example, your wife helps you by taking telephone messages or acting as your part-time assistant or secretary pay her a proper wage for these services. What you pay her can count as an expense in your accounts. She can then set off her wife's earned income relief against her wages. If these are less than £2,028 a year there will be no tax or National Insurance to pay on them. There will be some items of expenditure, such as a car used both privately and in your business, when it will be difficult to differentiate precisely between the private and business elements of the expenditure. Where there is this overlap you should agree the proportion which relates to your business with the Inland Revenue. If you do your office work from home you can include as a deduction in your accounts a proportion of your home expenses, such as rates, light, heat and insurance. Remember that if part of your home is used exclusively for business purposes, then should you come to sell your house the profit on sale attributable to that part will *not* be exempt from Capital Gains Tax.

Illustration
Jim White is a successful greengrocer who has just taken on a second shop.

In addition to the normal High Street trade, he supplies some of the local hotels on credit. One of these has gone out of business and Jim lost £190.

During the year Jim spent £1,300 on fixtures and fittings — including cash registers — for his new shop. He also bought another van for £5,500, and was allowed £1,000 for his old van in part exchange. He uses the family car partly for business, and keeps his account books and deals with business correspondence at home.

Jim White — Greengrocer

Income and Expenditure Account for the year ended 31 May 1987

EXPENDITURE	£			INCOME	£
Stock of produce at 1/6/86	100			Cash received from customers	120,000
Purchases during the year	89,600				
	89,700			Add: Outstanding accounts at year-end	1,500
Less: Stock of produce 31/5/87	180				121,500
		89,520		Less: Accounts outstanding beginning of year	800
Shop expenses:					120,700
Rent & rates	3,190				
Light & heat	510				
Insurance	265				
Repairs to glass frontage	130				
Cleaning	250				
		4,345			
Staff wages		11,760			
Wages to wife as part-time shop assistant		1,400			

Car & van expenses:	Car	Van	
Tax & insurance	180	230	
Petrol & oil	360	460	
Repairs & servicing	120	—	
Parking	—	80	
	660	770	
Business proportions	25%	100%	935

Use of home as office:		
Rates	480	
Light & heat	445	
Insurance	95	
	1,020	
Business proportion	1/6th	170
Telephone:		
Shop	160	
Home (50%)	70	
		230
Postage & stationery		80
Advertising		290
Subscription to local Chamber of Commerce		30
Entertaining		90
Legal expenses:		
Collection of bad debt	135	
Lease on new shop	460	
		595
Bad debt		190
Donations		15
		109,650
Profit for the year		11,050
		£120,700

£120,700

Computation of profits

It does not follow that the profit shown by your business accounts is the same as the one on which you pay tax. This is because some items of expenditure are specifically not deductible in computing your taxable business profits. Two types of expenditure which come into this category are business entertainment, unless it relates to overseas customers, and expenditure on items of a capital, as opposed to revenue, nature.

Illustration
Although Jim White's accounts for the year to 31 May 1987 show a profit of £11,050 his taxable profits are £11,615, as follows:

		£
Profit as per accounts		11,050
Add Disallowable expenses:		
Legal expenses for new lease	460	
Entertainment	90	
Donations	15	
		565
Profit as adjusted for tax purposes		£11,615

Assessment of profits

Your tax assessment is based on the profits for the accounting year which ended in the preceding year of assessment. For example, the profits from Jim White's greengrocery business for the year to 31 May 1987 will be taxed in 1988/89. The tax will be payable in two equal instalments on 1 January and 1 July 1989.

Where a new trade or business is set up, the assessments for more than one tax year are governed by the results for the first period of trading.

Illustration
Had Jim White only started trading as a greengrocer on 1 June 1986 his results for the year to 31 May 1987 would have formed the basis of his assessment for the first three years, as follows:

1986/87
Profits earned in year of assessment —
10/12ths × profits in year to 31 May 1987   £9,679

1987/88
Profits of first year's trading —
year to 31 May 1987   £11,615

1988/89
Profits shown by accounts ending in the
preceding year of assessment —
year to 31 May 1987   £11,615

Where it is advantageous the taxpayer can elect that the assessments for both the second and third years, but not only one of them, be adjusted to the actual profits earned in those years.

Tax saver If you ever set up in business choose carefully the date to mark the end of your accounting year. It can often afford an opportunity to minimize the Income Tax payable during the early stages of a new business. As a general guide select a date shortly after 5 April, such as the end of each April or May — Jim White chose the latter.

Where a business ceases to function, the assessment for the final year will be based on the profits from 6 April up to the date of cessation. The Inland Revenue has the option to adjust the assessments for the two years, but not only one of them, prior to the year in which cessation takes place. The assessments are revised to the actual profits earned in those years where this is to the Inland Revenue's advantage.

Capital allowances

Although you cannot deduct expenditure on items of a capital nature directly from your business profits, you do receive allowances for them. They are known as capital allowances. Generally, the total allowances due for a year of assessment are measured by the capital transactions of your business in the accounting year which forms the basis of the assessment.

Expenditure on machinery, equipment, motor vans, fixtures and fittings, and motor cars qualifies for a writing-down allowance of 25% per annum, commencing with the year of purchase. Thereafter the annual allowance of 25% is calculated on the balance after deduction of previous allowances. For cars costing more than £8,000 there is a maximum allowance of £2,000 per annum.

A separate 'pool' of expenditure must be maintained for each of these different categories, as follows:

(1) Plant and equipment, including motor vans and lorries

(2) Cars costing up to £8,000

(3) Each car bought for over £8,000

(4) Each asset used for both personal and business use

Where an asset on which capital allowances have been given is sold, such as Jim White's old van, the proceeds of sale must come into the computation of capital allowances. This can sometimes lead to a further allowance where an asset is sold for less than its written-down value for tax purposes. Alternatively, if it fetches an amount greater than its written-down value this can often mean that part of the allowances already given need to be withdrawn. These adjustments are respectively referred to as balancing allowances and balancing charges.

Illustration

Jim White's claim to capital allowances for 1988/89 based on his capital expenditure in the year to 31 May 1987 is:

	Pool £	Car with private use £
Written down values brought forward from 1987/88	1,100	4,400
Less: Sale proceeds of van	1,000	
	100	
Additions in the year:		
New van	5,500	
Equipment	1,300	
	6,900	
Allowances due:		
Writing down — 25%	1,725	1,100
Carried forward to 1989/90	£5,175	£3,300
Summary of allowances:		
Writing down	2,825	
Less: 75% private use of car	825	
1988/89 Capital allowances	£2,000	

Losses

Most businesses cannot escape going through a bad spell at some stage in their existence. Where the results of the business for the year show a loss you will be able to claim tax relief on the loss as increased by the amount of any claim to capital allowances. The overall loss is set against your other taxable income for the same year — which will include the profits from your business for the previous accounting year. Any unused part of the loss can then be set against your taxable income in the subsequent year. The balance of the loss which is left over must be carried forward to be set against the profits from the same business in later years.

There is a set procedure for setting off the loss. It must first of all reduce your other earned income for the year, then your unearned income, followed by your wife's earned income and finally her unearned income.

Loss relief against other income must be claimed by sending an election to your tax office within two years after the end of the tax year in which it arises.

Illustration
A trader suffered a loss of £4,500 in his business for the year ended 31 March 1988. His claim to capital allowances for the year is £2,400. His own and his wife's investment incomes for 1987/88 were £500 and £300 respectively.
In the previous year to 31 March 1987 the trader's taxable profits were £5,300.

The total business loss is:

	£
Trading loss	4,500
Capital allowances	2,400
	£6,900

This is set off as follows:

	£
Profits for the year to 31 March 1987 — taxed in 1987/88	5,300
Investment income — husband	500
— wife	300
1987/88 Loss relief claim	£6,100

The unrelieved loss of £800 can either be set off against the couple's income in 1988/89 or carried forward against future profits from the same business in later years.

If the end of your financial year does not coincide with the tax year, the loss should be split on a time basis between the tax years into which it falls.

Illustration
A trader incurred a loss of £3,000 in his business in the year to 31 December 1987. This will be apportioned as follows:

1986/87: 3/12ths × £3,000	750
1987/88: 9/12ths × £3,000	2,250
	£3,000

Alternatively where the loss arises in an established business the Inland Revenue will usually allocate the loss to the tax year in which the financial year ends. **Tax saver**

There is an alternative form of loss relief available for new businesses. It allows losses incurred during the first four years of assessment to be set against your income in the three years prior to that in which the loss arises. Relief is first of all given against your income for the earliest year. For example, if you started out in business during 1987/88 and incur a loss in the first period of trading the proportion attributable to the tax year 1987/88 can be set off against your income in 1984/85, 1985/86 and 1986/87, starting with 1984/85.

Frequently it is necessary to incur expenditure on a new business venture before it starts to trade. Any such expenditure incurred within three years prior to the commencement of trade is treated as a separate loss sustained in the tax year in which trading began.

Retirement annuities
As a self-employed person you will still want to provide yourself with a pension on retirement. The premiums you pay are allowed as a deduction from your profits. The maximum amount that you can contribute each year is expressed as a percentage of your taxable profits depending on your age:

Age at start of tax year	Percentage limit of profits %
Under 51	$17\frac{1}{2}$
51-55	20
56-60	$22\frac{1}{2}$
Over 60	$27\frac{1}{2}$

Up to 5% of your profits every year can be paid into a policy providing for the payment of a lump sum to your dependants in the event of your death. The lump sum would be free of Inheritance Tax. Premiums paid into this sort of policy count as part of the maximum permissible limit set out above.

Tax saver

Where you do not pay premiums up to the maximum permissible amount in any year the short-fall can be carried forward for up to six years. Relief outstanding for earlier years is used up before that still available for later years.

Illustration

A trader has been in business for many years. Since 1983/84 he has not been paying the maximum permissible premiums towards his pension, as follows:

Tax Year	Premiums Paid £	Maximum Permissible £	Shortfall £
1983/84	400	800	400
1984/85	450	840	390
1985/86	450	615	165
1986/87	500	735	235

During 1987/88 he paid premiums of £1,720; the maximum permissible premium limit for the year was £900. Nevertheless relief will be given for £1,720, as follows:

	£	£
Premium limit for 1987/88		900
Unused relief:		
1983/84	400	
1984/85	390	
1985/86 (part)	30	820
1987/88 Retirement annuity relief		£1,720

Premiums paid in the year can either be deducted from your taxable profits in the year of payment, or alternatively you can elect for them to be treated as if paid in the preceding year.

Although these policies are generally referred to as self-employed retirement annuities they can also be taken out by employees who are not members of their employer's pension scheme.

The Enterprise Allowance

The Enterprise Allowance is a weekly payment to individuals leaving the unemployment register to set up in business. The allowance is not treated as part of the takings of the recipient's business, although it is chargeable to Income Tax.

National Insurance

Like any employee you must pay National Insurance Contributions if you are self-employed. There are two rates. Class 2 is a weekly flat rate and Class 4 is based on a percentage of your business profits. If your earnings are below a specified limit you can be excempted from payment of Class 2 contributions. Table 4 at the end of the book sets out the rates for both Classes.

Half the amount of your Class 4 National Insurance contributions is allowed as a deduction in calculating your total income for each tax year, as follows:

Illustration

A trader's taxable profits after capital allowances for the year ended 30 September 1986 were £14,820. The Class 4 deduction from total income for 1987/88 is:

$$(£14,820 - £4,590) = £10,230 \times 6.3\% \times \tfrac{1}{2} = £322$$

Special situations

In the space available it has only been possible for me to paint a general picture of the way in which business profits are taxed. If you are a Lloyds underwriter, farmer, writer or subcontractor in the construction industry you should be aware that there are special rules which apply in calculating the tax on the profits from your trade or profession.

The letting of holiday accommodation in the U.K. is now treated as a trade. The accommodation has to be furnished residential property which is available for renting by the public as holiday accommodation for at least 140 days during each tax year. It must actually be let for a minimum of 70 days. There are other requirements which also need to be satisfied. Capital gains on disposals of holiday accommodation falling within these rules qualify for the replacement and retirement reliefs which apply to business assets (see Chapter 10).

There are also a number of specific rules which apply to the taxation of the profits of a partnership and in determining each individual partner's share of the partnership assessment. In these and other situations it is advisable to seek professional assistance in dealing with the tax affairs of the business concerned.

6

INVESTMENT INCOME

Most of you will at some time or other need to look into the various types of investment on offer. Perhaps you will be looking to find a suitable home for regular savings or to invest a more substantial amount such as an inheritance or a lump sum on retirement. As you no longer have to pay more tax on investment income it is now far less important to be able to distinguish it from earned income. Salaries, wages, directors' fees, business profits and pensions are examples of earned income. Investment or unearned income is that which does not depend on your active involvement or physical effort in some business or trade. Bank or building-society interest, dividends on shares or unit trust holdings, rents, income from a trust and interest on government stocks are all examples of investment income.

Investment income is subject to tax at both the basic and higher rates in the same way as earned income.

Tax-free income
The most widely known investments where the return is free of both Income Tax and Capital Gains Tax are some of those available from the Department for National Savings. They are:

Fixed Interest and Index-linked Savings Certificates   **Tax**
Yearly Savings Plan   **saver**
Premium Bond Prizes
First £70 of annual interest on a National Savings Bank
    Ordinary Account

Apart from interest on any National Savings account, no

details of these need to be shown on your annual Income Tax
Return.

Rental income

If you own a flat, house, shop or some other property which
you have let out to tenants you must show the rents and
expenses on your Tax Return. The Income Tax payable on your
net rental income is due on 1 January each year. For example,
the tax payable for 1987/88 was due on 1 January 1988. You
may well ask how the right amount of tax payable can be calculated when the exact amount of rental income is not known at
the time. The answer is that the Inspector of Taxes issues a pro-
visional assessment based on the agreed income for the previous year. This is adjusted when the current year's income is
ascertained.

Apart from expenditure of a capital nature, such as that on
structural alterations or improvements to a property, the general running costs of a property can be set against the rental
income.

Illustration

	£	£
Rent receivable from letting a house		4,800
Less: Expenses		
General rates	500	
Water rates	70	
Building insurance	90	
Redecorating two bedrooms	300	
Repairs to door locks and drains	150	
Agents fees for collecting rent	165	
		1,275
1987/88 Net rental income		£3,525

If you are letting a furnished property you can claim an additional deduction to cover the cost of wear and tear to furnish-
ings and fittings. This allowance is based on 10% of the rent
less the amount of the general and water rates. If the property
in the preceding illustration is let furnished this allowance
would be £423, as follows:

Illustration

Rent receivable	4,800
Less: General and water rates	570
	£4,230
Wear and tear allowance: 10%	£423

The rules dealing with the taxation of premiums on leases and the situations where losses arise on the letting of properties are more complicated and outside the scope of this book.

Dividends and interest

The table below sets out the types of investment where the dividends and interest are paid to the investor after deduction of Income Tax at the basic rate, together with those where no such deduction is made.

Tax deducted at source
Dividends on shares and unit trust holdings
Building society interest
Interest on British government stocks
Bank deposit interest

Interest not taxed at source
National Savings Bank ordinary and investment accounts
National Savings income and deposit bonds
Single deposits over £50,000 for a fixed period of more than 7 days
Deposits with non-U.K. branches of both U.K. and overseas banks

Many people mistakenly assume — because the dividends and interest mentioned in the first table are paid after tax at the basic rate has been deducted — that they need not be reported on their annual Tax Return. This misunderstanding is most particularly associated with building society interest. Whatever the amount of your dividends and interest these details must be shown on your Tax Return. You may be entitled to a tax repayment or the size of this income may be such as to give rise to a liability to tax at the higher rates.

Always remember that you can never recover the notional tax deducted from bank or building society interest. This can be of particular relevance to taxpayers living on low fixed incomes. Where their total income is below their personal allowances they will be able to recover any Income Tax paid providing none of their income comes from a bank or building society.

Interest on the various National Savings bonds or accounts in the second table above is taxed in a special way similar to the income or profits from self-employment. Where an account has been in existence for at least three years the interest earned in a tax year is the amount on which tax is paid in the following year. However, there are special rules for determining the interest which is taxable — not only in the early years after a new account is opened, but also in the final years before one is closed.

Illustration
A National Savings Bank investment account was opened in November 1985. The interest received and taxable amounts are:

Interest Received		Tax	Interest	
Date	Amount £	Year	Taxable £	Comments
Dec. 85	50	1985/86	50	Interest received in the tax year
Dec. 86	600	1986/87	600	Actual interest in the year
Dec. 87	500	1987/88	600	Interest for the previous tax year

Tax saver The taxpayer can elect for the interest taxable in the third year — 1987/88 — to be adjusted to the actual interest received in the year. In the above illustration the taxpayer would exercise this option and the taxable amount would be reduced to £500.

Illustration
A National Savings Bank Investment Account is closed in August 1988. The interest credited in the final years and the amounts taxable are:

Interest Received		Tax	Interest	
Date	Amount £	Year	Taxable £	Comments
Dec. 86	500	1986/87	525	Interest received in the previous year
Dec. 87	450	1987/88	500	Previous year's interest
Aug. 88	300	1988/89	300	Actual interest received in the year

The Inland Revenue can alter the amount of the assessment in the penultimate year — 1987/88 — to the actual interest received in the year. Clearly in the above illustration this would not be to their advantage as it would reduce the interest taxable from £500 to £450.

As with income from property, Income Tax on untaxed interest is payable on each 1 January.

Accrued income

Interest on fixed-rate investments is treated as accruing on a day-to-day basis between payment dates. On a sale the vendor is charged to Income Tax on the accrued interest from the previous payment date to the date of the transaction. The purchaser is allowed to deduct this amount from the interest which he receives on the following payment date. These arrangements cover both fixed and variable-rate stocks and bonds, including those issued by governments, companies and local authorities. The arrangements will not affect you if the nominal value of your securities is under £5,000. This limit applies jointly to husband and wife.

Illustration
The interest on a holding of 12% Treasury Stock 1995 is payable on each 25 January and 25 July. The half-yearly interest on a holding of £20,000, sold for settlement on 8 May 1987, is £1,200.

$$\text{Accrued proportion} = \frac{103}{181} \times £1,200 = £682.87$$

Single premium bonds

Guaranteed income bonds and investment bonds offered by most insurance companies fall within this category. A lump sum premium is paid at the outset. The investor can usually either draw an income from the bond or leave it untouched until it is subseqently cashed in. No tax relief is due on the single premium. The proceeds of a single premium bond are not liable to Capital Gains Tax or Income Tax at the basic rate.

There can be a liability to tax at the higher rates on the profit element, depending on the level of the investor's income in the tax year the bond is encashed. The method of calculating the additional Income Tax due on the gain from a single premium bond involves a number of stages.

Illustration

A married man invested £10,000 in a single premium bond in 1982. He cashed it in during 1987 for £16,000. His income for 1987/88 was £24,675, of which £15,175 was earned and £9,500 was investment income.

Gain on encashment of bond	£6,000
Number of years held	5
Taxable slice of gain	£1,200

Taxable Income	£
Earnings	15,175
Investment income	9,500
Slice of gain	1,200
	25,875
Less: Personal allowance	3,795
	£22,080

Tax payble thereon excluding slice of gain:		
First £17,900 at 27%		4,833
Next £2,500 at 40%		1,000
Next £480 at 45%		216
£20,880		£6,049

Slice of gain of £1,200 will attract a tax rate of	45%

Therefore the rate of tax to apply to the gain is:
45% — 27% (basic rate) = 18%

The tax payable on the gain = £6,000 at 18% = £1,080

Personal equity plans

Tax saver From the beginning of 1987 all individuals over 18 have been allowed to invest up to £2,400 per annum on a calendar-year basis in a personal equity plan (PEP). The funds in a PEP must be invested in ordinary shares of a company incorporated in the U.K. and quoted on a U.K. stock exchange or dealt in on the Unlisted Securities Market. Investments in an investment or authorized unit trust are allowed but they must not exceed the greater of £420 and one quarter of the cash subscribed under the plan. Provided the plan is held for a minimum period of between 12 months and two years any capital gains and dividends within a PEP will be entirely free of tax. The proceeds from selling shares and dividend income received may be retained within a PEP and used to buy further shares over and above the annual limit of £2,400.

If you withdraw your investment before the minimum period has elapsed you will lose the tax reliefs and any capital gains and dividend income will be taxed in the usual way.

Forestry

Investing in woodlands on a commercial basis with a view to profit is likely to be of great interest to the high taxpayer. You can send an election to the Inland Revenue requiring your woodlands plantation to be taxed as if it were a business. This enables all the costs of planting, management and interest on money borrowed to finance the purchase of the land to be off-set against your other income. Once you have made this election you can never switch back to the alternative basis of being taxed on just a nominal value representing the annual value of the land. Ideally, you would want to do this just before the woodlands mature and you come to sell the timber from the felled trees. To overcome this difficulty you can either sell the plantation or, for example, transfer the woodlands down to your children. If you do this the overall result is that the earlier losses on the planting and maintenance expenditure qualify for tax relief whereas the subsequent profits from the sale of the timber are tax free.

Tax saver

Business Expansion Scheme

The concept of granting tax relief on minority investments in

Tax saver

new companies was introduced in 1981 under the umbrella of the Business Start-Up Scheme. Commencing with the tax year 1983/84 changes have been made to the original scheme to make it more attractive to potential investors. Nevertheless there are still many conditions which must be met both by the individual and the company whose shares are being acquired.

The scheme is now known as the Business Expansion Scheme. The maximum amount that an individual may now invest in additional ordinary shares in new or established trading companies whose shares are not quoted on a recognized stock exchange or dealt in on the Unlisted Securities Market is £40,000 per year. The minimum investment limit is £500 per annum. For a married couple living together, these limits apply to them jointly. The income tax relief is given by deducting the cost of shares subscribed for from the investor's total income in the year during which they are issued. Investors can claim relief on up to one half of the cost of investments made in the first half of a tax year against income of the previous tax year. The carry-back is limited to a maximum of £5,000. The balance of the relief is allowed in the year during which the investments were actually made. If Business Expansion Scheme investments are disposed of within five years the tax relief can be reduced or withdrawn. Because of the numerous restrictions the most suitable way of taking advantage of this relief could be through one of the many special investment funds now formed for this purpose.

7

THE FAMILY UNIT

The concept of the family unit has long been the framework around which our tax system is built. Unless the married couple elect to be separately assessed, responsibility for completing the annual Tax Return rests with the husband. There are situations, such as a wife earning a salary subject to PAYE, when she pays tax on her income. Otherwise it is the husband who has to pay the tax on the couple's joint income. However, if he fails to pay his tax the wife can then be asked to pay the tax due on her income.

Although children are part of the family unit they are treated as separate individuals for tax purposes. For this reason I have devoted a whole chapter (Chapter 8) to the position of children in our tax system.

Marriage
It is a general principle that the incomes of husband and wife be joined together to calculate the tax payable by the married couple. The first time this happens is the tax year following that in which they are married. For example, a couple whose wedding was in July 1987 will be taxed as single persons for 1987/88. Their incomes will first be aggregated in 1988/89.

Beginning with the year of marriage the husband is entitled to the married man's personal allowance. This was referred to in Chapter 2.

Separate assessment
Unlike the separate taxation of a wife's earnings there is no saving in tax from separate assessment. It is only helpful for

the couple who wish to maintain some degree of privacy from one another in their financial affairs. The election to be separately assessed can be made by either husband or wife. It must be in writing and be made within the six months prior to 5 July in the tax year when it is intended to come into effect. For example, an election for separate assessment for 1988/89 must be sent to the Inland Revenue at any time in the six months up to 5 July 1988. Once it has been made, the election stays in operation until it is withdrawn within the same time limit.

Under a separate assessment election husband and wife each complete their own Tax Returns in the same way as if they were still single. They are also responsible for paying the tax due on their respective incomes. It is down to the Inland Revenue to work this out. After the two Tax Returns have been received the tax payable on the joint income is calculated and the total is apportioned between husband and wife in ratio to their income.

Illustration

	Joint £	Husband £	Wife £
Earned income	24,100	13,900	10,200
Investment income	3,300	2,500	800
	27,400	16,400	11,000
Less: Mortgage interest	2,000	2,000	—
Taxable income before allowances	£25,400	£14,400	£11,000

Income Tax thereon:	8,083		
Divisible:			
Husband $\dfrac{14,400}{25,400} \times 8,083$		4,582.49	
Wife $\dfrac{11,000}{25,400} \times 8,083$			3,500.51

Personal allowance	3,795		
Wife's earned income allowance	2,425		
Apportioned 4,582:3,501	£6,220	£3,526	£2,694

Relief in terms of tax
  for personal allowances

£5,000 at 45%	2,250	1,275.48	974.52
£1,220 at 40%	488	276.64	211.36
	2,738.00	1,552.12	1,185.88
1986/87 Tax payable under separate assessment	£5,345.00	£3,030.37	£2,314.63

The calculations can be even more involved when the couple's income comes from a number of sources and they are claiming various deductions and reliefs. Where the wife has earned income her share of the allowances must never drop below the allowance on this earned income.

Separate taxation of wife's earnings

A saving in tax can be achieved when a married couple make this election. Whether it benefits them depends on both the level of their joint income and the amount of the wife's earned income. This can be either a salary, profits from a business, or her own pension. What happens when an election is made is that the wife's earned income is separated from the couple's other income and is taxed separately. Their other income, including any income from the wife's investments, is still taxed on the husband.

Tax saver

The husband loses the married man's allowance and receives the single allowance instead. Before the husband and wife can benefit from making the election they must be able to reduce their tax payable at the higher rates by an amount at least equivalent to that on the loss of the married man's allowance.

The couple's allowances and reliefs are allocated in the same way as if they were still single persons. The relief for mortgage interest payments is given to the borrower. Where there is a joint mortgage the relief will be given to the spouse who makes the repayments to the bank or building society. When an election is in force it can sometimes be to the couple's advantage for the wife to pay part or all of the interest on a joint mortgage.

It is not possible to generalize on the income level needed before a saving in tax is achieved by making this election. Every couple should do their own calculations. Where the deductions from their income are confined to their personal allowances, their joint income must be at least £26,869 for 1987/88. At this income level, the wife's earned income must come to more than £6,544, as must the husband's income from all sources, both earned and unearned.

	Joint		Separate		
			Husband		Wife
		£		£	£
Earned income		32,000		20,000	12,000
Investment income					
Husband		2,500		2,500	
Wife		500		500	
		35,000		23,000	12,000
Less:					
Personal allowance	3,795		2,425		
Wife's earned income allowance	2,425			2,425	
Mortgage interest	2,000	8,220	2,000	4,425	2,425
Taxable income		£26,780		£18,575	£9,575
Income tax thereon					
at 27%	17,900	4,833	17,900	4,833.00	9,575	2,585.25
at 40%	2,500	1,000	675	270.00	
at 45%	5,000	2,250			
at 50%	1,380	690			
		£8,773		£5,103.00	2,585.25
					£7,688.25

1987/88 Saving in tax from a wife's earnings election   £1,084.75

An election for the separate taxation of a wife's earnings must be made jointly by both husband and wife. It can be made at any time in the period beginning six months before and

Where the wife receives all the maintenance

		£
Payments under court order		10,000
Less: Personal allowance	2,425	
Additional personal allowance	1,370	
		3,795
Taxable Income		£6,205
Income Tax thereon at 27%		£1,675.35

Where the maintenance is split between wife and children

	Wife £	Child 1 £	Child 2 £
Payments under court order	7,000	1,500	1,500
Less: Personal allowance	2,425	2,425	2,425
Additional personal allowance	1,370		
	3,795		
	£3,205	Nil	Nil
Income Tax thereon at 27%	£865.35		

1987/88 Reduction in Income Tax payable £810

Old age

Unfortunately, the elderly taxpayer has to cope with the tax system in exactly the same way as the rest of us. Nevertheless, there are some factors which are only relevant in calculating the tax payable on the elderly person's income. The first of these is the age allowance. In Chapter 2 I explained how a pensioner calculates whether he or she is entitled to this allowance.

Apart from the war widow's pension, a pension from either the State or a past employer's pension fund is taxable. A wife's pension based on her own past contributions attracts the wife's earned income relief. Although it is taxable, no tax is deducted at source from the National Insurance Pension. A pension from a former employer's pension scheme is taxed under PAYE. In addition to including the pensioner's personal allowances the coding notice will incorporate a deduction equivalent to the State retirement pension. In this way the tax due on it is collected. The necessity of a direct payment of tax is avoided.

Illustration

	£
Pension from former employer	4,286
National Insurance pension	3,289
	7,575
Less: Married age allowance (age 65—79)	4,675
Taxable income	£2,900
Code number based on:	
Age allowance	4,675
Less: State Pension	3,289
	£1,386

Code allocated: 138V

A code number ending with the letter V indicates the pensioner is entitled to the married age allowance. A coding which includes the single age allowance finishes up with the letter P. In the exceptional situation of the deduction for the State Retirement Pension exceeding the pensioner's personal allowances, the Inland Revenue issue an F coding. This is an instruction to apply a special rate of tax in calculating the deductions under PAYE on the pension from a previous employer's pension fund. Nevertheless, there will still be some circumstances where it is just not possible to collect all the tax due on the elderly taxpayer's pensions under PAYE. Then it is necessary for the tax office to issue an assessment. The tax payable will be due in four equal instalments.

When a person retires and starts to draw the old age pension, the Department of Health and Social Security send out a form to find out the tax office which deals with the pensioner's Tax Return. The purpose behind this is to enable the Department to tell the new pensioner's tax office of the amount of his or her National Insurance Pension and each subsequent increase. This will help make sure the correct deduction for the State pension is always included in the pensioner's code number.

If you have an elderly relative living on a low fixed income who you are helping to support you should consider doing this by deed of covenant (see Chapter 3). Although it is outside the scope of this book, elderly people can often obtain housing or other benefits from the Department of Health and Social Security.

Death

Sadly, death comes to all of us sooner or later. Needless to say it also has some consequences so far as taxation is concerned. From the date of death the surviving spouse is again taxable as a single person. When death occurs midway through a tax year the widow is entitled to set her allowances against whatever income she receives in the rest of the year. In addition, she can claim the widow's bereavement allowance (see Chapter 2). In the year of death the husband is taxed on the couple's joint income up to the date of death. He does not lose his entitlement to the married man's allowance for that year.

If the wife dies first the husband can disclaim liability for any tax due on her income for the tax year in which death takes place. This will then have to be met by her executors out of her estate.

8

CHILDREN

Like you or I a child is a potential taxpayer so far as the various taxes on income and capital are concerned. The Income Tax liability of a minor child is calculated in exactly the same way as that for anyone else. A child is entitled to the single personal allowance. If he is married he can claim the higher married man's allowance. If all this tempts you to think about giving some of your savings to your children so that the Income Tax on the interest or dividends can be recovered by set-off against their personal allowances then I must warn you to proceed with caution. The income from a gift by a parent in favour of an unmarried minor child is still regarded as the parent's income for tax purposes if it is paid out or applied for the child's benefit. If the income is accumulated it will be treated as belonging to the child. Neither income nor capital should be used until the child is 18. Grandparents or other relatives can, however, transfer some of their income over to their grandchildren or nieces, nephews, etc., without the same restrictions. This is most commonly done under a deed of covenant, which is dealt with later on in this chapter. Responsibility for completing a minor's Income Tax Repayment Claim rests with a child's trustee or guardian.

A minor child is also a taxable person for the purposes of Capital Gains Tax (see Chapter 10) and Inheritance Tax (see Chapter 14).

Allowances and benefits
There is no longer any general tax allowance for children. You will probably be able to claim the additional personal allow-

ance if you are single and have a child living with you (see Chapter 2).

The tax allowance for children was replaced by Child Benefit. Generally, this is payable to the mother. The present rate is £7.25 per week for each child. It is not taxable. Depending on your personal circumstances you may be entitled to one or more of the numerous other Social Security Benefits associated with children, but unfortunately it is outside the scope of this book to detail them.

Investment of savings

Most parents will usually opt for either a building society or bank deposit account when investing their child's savings. In the chapter on investment income (Chapter 6) I compared the payment of interest on a National Savings Bank investment account, where tax is not deducted at source, with that paid on a bank or building society account. Here the interest is paid to the investor after deduction of tax at the basic rate. This can never be recovered even if your child's income is beneath the level of his or her personal allowance. Accordingly, you should compare the gross rate of interest on a National Savings Bank investment account with a net rate on either a bank or building society account when deciding which offers the best return for your child's savings.

The various other types of National Savings can also be used for the investment of children's savings. An added attraction is their degree of security.

Deeds of covenant

These are by far the most common way of giving a child a tax free income up to the level of the single personal allowance. The general conditions which must be satisfied for a deed of covenant to be valid were set out in Chapter 3. There are two main occasions when a not insignificant saving in Income Tax can be achieved by executing a deed of covenant in favour of a child.

Tax saver

The first is when the child is still a minor. This is where the generous grandparent or other relation, except the parent, can help. The annual amount payable under the deed can be used by the parents for the general education and wellbeing of the child. This may be particularly helpful for parents whose children are being privately educated. Where the child is still a minor the covenant should be drawn up in favour of trustees, usually the parants, for the child's benefit.

Illustration

THIS DEED OF COVENANT is made the [date of deed] between [name of person making covenant] of [address of person making covenant] (hereinafter called 'the Grantor') of the one part and [name of first trustee] of [address of first trustee] and [name of second trustee] of [address of second trustee] (hereinafter called 'the Trustees') of the other part.

THIS DEED WITNESSETH AS FOLLOWS:

1. The Grantor hereby covenants with the Trustees that the Grantor will pay to the Trustees [date of payment] in each year for the period of seven years or the period of the joint lives of the Grantor and [name of child beneficiary] of [address of child] (hereinafter called 'the Beneficiary') whichever period shall be the shorter the gross sum of [gross annual amount of covenant] the first payment to be made on the [the date of first payment].

2. The Trustees shall hold the said sums upon trust for the Beneficiary absolutely.

3. The power of appointment of new or additional Trustees shall be vested in the Grantor during his/her lifetime.

IN WITNESS whereof the parties hereto have hereunto set their hands and seals the date and year first before written.

Signed, sealed and delivered by
the said [name of person making   [signature of person making   [seal]
covenant]   covenant]
in the presence of:
[name and address of witness]

Signed, sealed and delivered by
the said [name of first trustee]   [signature of first trustee] [seal]
in the presence of:
[name and address of witness]

Signed, sealed and delivered by
the said [name of second trustee]   [signature of second trustee] [seal]
in the presence of:
[name and address of witness]

Where, for example, the gross amount covenanted by a grandparent is £1,500 he or she deducts Income Tax at 27% of £405 from each annual payment to the child's trustees. They receive £1,095 from the grandparent and the remaining £405 from the Inland Revenue. To give the child £1,500 only costs the grandparent £1,095.

Illustration

	Income £	Tax £
Annual payment under deed of covenant	1,500	405
Less: Personal allowance	2,425	
Taxable income	Nil	Nil
Tax repayable		£405

Providing the grandparent has sufficient income each year taxable at the basic rate to cover the gross amount payable under the covenant, his or her Income Tax position should be unaffected. In view of the various exemptions set out in Chapter 14 a charge to Inheritance Tax on the amount of the covenant is unlikely to arise.

The second and more popular use of a deed of covenant is that taken out by a parent in favour of a child of his or hers who is either over 18 or married and still in full-time education. This type of covenant is commonly known as a student deed of covenant. As a covenant must be capable of exceeding a period of six years to be valid for tax purposes, this condition must still be included in the deed. However, as the deed is really only intended to cover the period until the adult student ceases full-time education this additional factor also needs to be mentioned. Even though a period of further education at a university or college is unlikely to last for more than four years, it is conceivable that it could go on for longer and, therefore, the extra wording does not invalidate the deed. It will frequently be attractive for the annual amount under a deed to be payable in instalments to coincide, for example, with the beginning of each term at college or university. As a help to parents the

Inland Revenue has issued an acceptable form of wording for a deed of covenant by a parent to an adult student. This is contained in Form IR47. In addition to setting out the procedure to be followed and the points to note the form contains a specimen deed of covenant, as follows:

Illustration

To be completed by a Covenantor (Parent) resident in England, Wales or Northern Ireland.

DEED OF COVENANT
I [name of person making covenant]
of [address of person making covenant]
covenant to pay my son/daughter [full name of child]
of [address of child]
the sum of £...... (gross) on
[state date or dates] in each year, for the period of seven years, or for the period of our joint lives, or until he/she ceases to be receiving full-time education at any university, college, school or other educational establishment (whichever is the shortest period) the first payment to be made on
.... Date ....

Signed, sealed and delivered by
[signature of person making covenant]
in the presence of [witness's signature and address]
Person making the covenant

Please state below the Tax District (and reference number) which deals with your tax affairs
District .... Reference ....

More recently the Inland Revenue have brought out a new publication — IR59 — which is a Student's Tax Information Pack. In addition to incorporating the form containing a specimen deed of covenant it includes the following:

IR60	Income Tax and Students
IR61	Student Deeds of Covenant
IR61A	Student Deeds of Covenant — how to fill in the forms
Form R40(S)	Tax Repayment Claim for Students
Form R110(1985)	Certificates to be completed by Covenantor and Covenantee
Form R185 (AP) New	Certificate of Deduction of Income Tax

Providing the adult student's other income is less than his or her personal allowance, all or part of the Income Tax deducted by the parent is repayable.

The income received under deed of covenant is not counted in assessing the amount of any educational grant to which the student may be entitled.

Payments under court order
We have already seen in Chapter 7 that on the breakdown of a marriage a considerable saving in tax can often be achieved by structuring the amount of maintenance payable by the husband in such a way that a proportion is paid to his children. They then claim their personal allowances against the court order payments.

9

THE OVERSEAS ELEMENT

So far we have only been concerned with the tax position of
individuals permanently resident in the United Kingdom. In
this chapter I shall concentrate on some of the opportunities
for tax planning which present themselves to those persons
taking up employment overseas and to those individuals
coming to work in the U.K.

Domicile and residence

The two concepts of domicile and residence are of fundamental
importance in determining the extent of an individual's liability to U.K. taxation. Their significance is not just confined to
Income Tax but also to Capital Gains Tax and Inheritance Tax.

Whereas your residence status is dependent upon physical
presence in the U.K., your domicile will generally be the country or state which you regard as your permanent homeland.
For the majority of people this is their country of birth. You can
abandon your original domicile by birth if you settle in another
country or state with a view to making it your new permanent
home. Providing you sever all links with the country where
you were born you will acquire a domicile of choice in the new
country. A wife's domicile is not dependent on that of her
husband if they were married at some time after the end of
1973. Prior to that time a wife's domicile was the same as her
husband's.

If you think you have good grounds for believing that you
should not be regarded as domiciled in the U.K. you should
write to your tax office about this. Usually, you can then expect
to receive a questionnaire which you should fill in and send

back to your tax office. The information you have supplied will be considered by the Inland Revenue's Specialist Department which deals with these matters before you are given a ruling on your status. Later on in this chapter we shall see how much more favourably individuals not domiciled in the U.K. are taxed on their overseas earnings and investment income.

All of you that permanently live and work in the U.K. are regarded as both resident and ordinarily resident for the purposes of U.K. taxation. Whenever you go abroad for just short periods your residence status is unaffected.

A visitor to this country will generally not become resident here unless the stay in a tax year lasts longer than six months. If on the other hand the visitor establishes a pattern of regular visits, U.K. residence will usually be established when the average time spent here comes to at least ninety days a year over a four year period.

Should the overseas visitor have a home in the U.K. which is available for his or her use the visitor will be resident here every year in which he or she sets foot in the U.K. This does not apply if the visitor is engaged in some full-time occupation overseas.

Going non-resident

The dual incentives of high salaries and low taxation may prompt you to decide to apply for a job overseas. This may involve living permanently abroad for a time. Your likely residence status is clearly set out in paragraph 18 of the Inland Revenue booklet IR20 — 'Residents and Non-Residents Liability to Tax in the United Kingdom' — as follows:

'If a person goes abroad for full-time service under a contract of employment and:

(a) All the duties of his employment are performed abroad or any duties he performs here are incidental to his duties abroad; and

(b) His absence from the U.K. and the employment itself both extend over a period covering a complete tax year; and

(c) Any interim visits to the U.K. during the period do not amount to (i) 6 months or more in any one tax year, or (ii) an average of 3 months or more per tax year,

he is normally regarded as not resident and not ordinarily resident in the U.K. from the day following the date of his departure until the day preceding the date of his return. On his return he is regarded as a new permanent resident.'

Just before you depart to take up your overseas assignment, write to your tax office and tell them of your plans. You will be sent a Form P85 to complete. This will tell your tax office whether your overseas employment is full-time, where you will be staying abroad, and how long you expect to remain away. It also asks whether your wife is accompanying you and what, if any, income you will be receiving in the U.K. while you are abroad. For example, you might arrange to let your house until you come back. The income from the letting will be taxable in the U.K. The amount of income on which you will pay tax is calculated in the same way as that set out in Chapter 6.

If you take up an overseas employment part way through a tax year you will normally be due an Income Tax repayment. This is because you are entitled to a full year's personal allowances for the period up to the date of departure. By that time you will only have received a proportion of these in calculating the monthly deduction of PAYE from your salary.

Tax saver The astute would-be expatriate will realize that some of the potential opportunities for tax planning afforded by an overseas appointment need to be acted upon before departure. This is particularly so where the would-be expatriate is a married man and his wife is staying at home to look after their young children. While he becomes non-resident from the date of his departure she remains resident in the U.K. and reverts back to being taxed as a single person. Where she is looking after children she can also claim the additional personal allowance. If she does not work while her husband is abroad she will lose the benefit of her personal allowances unless she has some income against which to offset them. It is in these circumstances that the husband should transfer to his wife before he goes abroad those income-producing assets where she can reclaim the tax deducted from the income by set-off against her personal allowances. Generally, it is where the husband has a portfolio of shares that transfer of the ownership of these to his wife produces a more favourable tax treatment. This is because his dividend income will remain taxable in the U.K. while he is abroad. At best he would only be able to reclaim part of the tax back under a Double Tax Agreement between the United Kingdom and his new country of residence, and claim a proportion of his U.K. personal allowances in the ratio that his income liable to U.K. tax bears to his total world income.

As a general guide you will not have to pay U.K. tax on any overseas income you receive while you are abroad. You might choose to invest part of your savings in one of the many U.K. Government Securities where the interest is free of U.K. tax when owned by a non-resident. So long as you remain classified as non-resident you can also invest in a U.K. bank or building society and earn gross interest on the amount invested. **Tax saver**

Before you return to take up U.K. residence again there are some specific tax-planning points which must be considered. For example, any deposit or building society accounts should be closed before you return as you could otherwise face the prospect of a charge to U.K. Income Tax on interest earned during your period of non-residence.

Taking up U.K. residence

If you have just arrived in this country you are probably anxious to know how much tax you will have to pay each year. In view of my comments at the beginning of the chapter you should initially be able to satisfy our Inland Revenue Authorities that you have an overseas domicile. Any income from investments here is taxable as it arises, but your overseas investment income is not taxed unless it is actually remitted here.

Where your job is with either a U.K. or overseas employer and the duties of your employment are performed wholly in the U.K., the full amount of your salary is taxable here. If you were working for a foreign employer in the U.K. before 14

March 1984 and have not been resident here for nine out of ten years prior to 1987/88 you are only taxed on 25% of your earnings in the U.K. You can of course claim any U.K. personal allowances to which you are entitled.

Illustration

A married couple, domiciled overseas, came to live in the U.K. in July 1983. The husband is employed by a foreign employer. His earnings during 1987/88 were £24,000. The U.K. Income Tax payable for the year amounts to £3,835.35, as follows:

	£
Earned income	24,000
Less: Deduction — 25%	6,000
	18,000
Personal allowance	3,795
Taxable income	£14,205

1987/88 Tax payable at 27% £3,835.35

While you live here you might still have to complete a Tax Return in your overseas country of origin and pay taxes there as well. If it is one of the countries which have concluded a Double Tax Agreement with the U.K. you should not have to pay tax twice on the same income.

10

CAPITAL GAINS TAX

True to its name, Capital Gains Tax is a tax on capital profits. As with most other forms of taxation there is the usual list of exceptions to this general rule. Gambling or pools winnings and personal or professional damages are not taxable. Neither are gains realized on disposing of any of the assets in the following table:

Private cars
National Savings
Your private residence
Chattels, with an expected life of more than fifty years, sold for less than £3,000
British government securities and corporate bonds
Shares issued under the Business Expansion Scheme after 18 March 1986 on their first disposal. For the exemption to apply, the Income Tax relief granted must not have been withdrawn.
Investments held for the minimum qualifying period in a personal equity plan
Life assurance policies
Charitable gifts
Gifts for the public benefit
Standing timber
Foreign currency for personal expenditure.

In addition, for the year 1987/88 the first £6,600 of chargeable gains are exempt from tax. The excess is charged at the flat rate of 30%. Like the main personal allowances the annual exemption limit goes up each year in line with the movement in the Retail Prices Index during the previous calendar year.

The indexation allowance

This allowance measures the impact of inflation on both the cost of an asset and any other expenditure incurred on enhancing its value. The rules dealing with the calculation of the allowance are:

(1) The allowance is governed by the movement in the Retail Prices Index in the period of ownership. For assets which you have owned since before April 1982 the starting date for calculating the indexation allowance is March 1982.

(2) When you dispose of an asset which you acquired before 6 April 1982 the indexation allowance can be calculated on either the market value of the asset at 31 March 1982 or its actual cost, whichever is the greater.

(3) The allowance will still be given where an asset is sold at a loss. The indexation allowance can also turn a gain into a loss.

Table 4 at the end of the book sets out the indexation allowance for assets disposed of between April and December 1987 that were acquired before the end of 1985.

Illustration
A property purchased in 1978 for £25,000 was sold in June 1987 for £75,000. At 31 March 1982 the property had a value of £32,000. The indexation allowance between March 1982 and June 1987 is 0.283.

The chargeable gain is calculated as follows:

	£	£
Proceeds of sale		75,000
Less: Purchase price	25,000	
Indexation allowance:		
£32,000 × 0.283	9,056	34,056
Chargeable gain		40,944

If the property had been bought in August 1982 the indexation allowance would be due from August 1982 up to the sale in June 1987.

Husband and wife

In the year of marriage husband and wife each remain taxable as single persons. Both of them can realize chargeable gains up to the limit of the exempt amount without incurring a charge to Capital Gains Tax. Thereafter the exemption limit of £6,600 is divisible between them on a pro rata basis depending on the gains they make in a tax year. Losses made by one spouse can be set against gains realized by the other in the same or subsequent years. Unless the couple elect for separate assessment for Capital Gains Tax the husband is responsible for paying the tax on both his own and his wife's gains. So long as the married couple are living together, assets can be transferred between them without incurring a charge to tax. The amount of any indexation allowance up to the time of transfer must be worked out. The calculation of the allowance due to the transferee on an eventual disposal of an asset is more complicated. When a couple permanently separate from one another the ability to transfer assets between them free of tax is lost.

The computation of gains

The taxable gain on the disposal of an asset is calculated by making various deductions from the price realized on sale, as follows:

(1) The cost of acquisition, and

(2) The incidental costs of buying and selling the asset, and

(3) Any additional expenditure incurred on enhancing the value of the asset during the period of ownership, and

(4) The indexation allowance.

There are occasions when a different figure from the actual disposal proceeds is substituted in the calculation. For example, this happens when you make a gift or sell an asset at a nominal value to a close member of your family. You must then bring into the computation of the capital gain the open-market value of the asset at the time of disposal.

The date of sale of an asset is taken as the date when the contract for sale is made.

Illustration

A property was purchased in 1979 for £30,000. The costs of purchase, including solicitor's fees and Stamp Duty, came to £1,100. In 1980 central heating was installed for £1,500. At 31 March 1982 the property had a market value of £40,000. Contracts for sale were exchanged in May 1987 and the sale was completed in July 1987. The property was sold for £80,000. The agent's commission amounted to £1,840 and the solicitor's fees came to £575. The indexation allowance between March 1982 and May 1987 is 0.283.

The chargeable gain is calculated as follows:

	£	£
Proceeds of sale		80,000
Less: Agent's and solicitor's fees		2,415
		77,585
Less: Purchase price	30,000	
Costs of purchase	1,100	
Expenditure on improvements	1,500	
	32,600	
Indexation allowance:		
£40,000 × 0.283	11,320	
		43,920
Chargeable gain		£33,665

Losses

Losses can be set against gains made in the same year. Where the result for the year is an overall loss it can be carried forward to be set against gains in a later year without time limit. It then reduces the amount of your gains which exceed the exemption limit, as follows:

Illustration

A taxpayer had capital losses of £1,860 available for carry-forward at 5 April 1987. During 1987/88 the taxpayer realized gains of £7,570 and made losses of £610.

The capital gains position for the year is:

	£	£
Gains realized in the year		7,570
Less: Losses: in the year	610	
brought forward (part)	360	
		970
1986/87 Exemption limit		£6,600

The unused losses of £1,500 can be carried forward to be set against gains in later years.

A loss arising on the sale or gift of an asset to a person connected with the transferor can only be set against a gain from a similar disposal at some time in the future. Where the value of an asset you own becomes negligible or nil you can claim the loss without actually disposing of the asset. If you have subscribed for shares in a trading company which are not quoted on a recognized stock exchange and you make a loss on selling them or they become worthless, you can set this loss against your income rather than against your other capital gains.

Tax saver

Your private residence

The profit on a sale of your home is exempt from tax. The exemption extends to the house and its garden or grounds up to one acre, including the land on which the house is built. A larger area can qualify for exemption where it can be shown that it was needed to enjoy the house. Where a home has not been occupied as your private residence throughout the full period of ownership, a proportion of the gain on sale becomes taxable. Nevertheless, certain periods of absence are disregarded in determining whether the gain is totally exempt from tax. These are the last twenty-four months of ownership in any event and generally those when you have to live away from home because of your work.

Where part of your home is used exclusively for business purposes the proportion of the profit on sale attributable to the business use is a chargeable gain. Whether part of your home is actually used exclusively for business use is entirely a matter of fact. If you let part of your home as residential accommodation the gain on the part which has been let is either wholly or partly exempt from tax. The proportion of the profit on sale which is exempt is the lower of either £20,000 or an amount equivalent to the gain on the part you have occupied as your home. Alternatively, if you take in lodgers who mix in and eat with your family, the Inland Revenue take the view that no part of the exemption on a sale of your home is lost.

A second home

If you have two homes such as a house or flat in town for use during the weekdays and a cottage in the country for weekends, the profit on sale of only one of them is exempt from tax. Which one counts as your main residence is a matter of fact. It is, however, possible for you to determine this by writing to your tax office. In the election you should request which of your homes you want to be regarded as your principal private residence for Capital Gains Tax purposes. The election can start to apply from any time in the two years up to the date it is made. You are, of course, free to vary it as and when it suits you. If you own a home which is occupied rent-free by a dependent relative then the profit on sale is tax-free.

Stocks and shares

Prior to 6 April 1982 each shareholding was regarded as a single asset. This was commonly known as a 'pool'. Each additional purchase of the same class of shares or a sale of part of the holding either represented an addition to, or a disposal out of, the pool. With the introduction of the indexation allowance this changed. Each shareholding acquired after 5 April 1982 represented a separate asset. A subsequent addition to a holding you owned at 5 April 1982 could not be added to the pool.

As from 6 April 1985 the rules have been altered once more. Shares of the same class are again regarded as a single asset growing or diminishing on each acquisition or disposal. This new form of 'pooling' applies to shares acquired after 5 April 1982 unless they had already been disposed of before 6 April 1985; it is called a 'new holding'. A pool which was frozen under the 1982 rules stays that way. It remains a single asset which cannot grow by subsequent acquisitions and is to be known as a '1982 holding'. The rules are even more complicated where you may still own any shares which were acquired before 6 April 1965. A '1982 holding' is treated like any other asset in calculating the indexation allowance. This is not so for a 'new holding'. It is to be kept continually indexed each time there is either an addition to or a disposal out of the pool.

The procedure for matching shares sold with their corresponding acquisition is as follows:

(1) Shares acquired on the same day.

(2) Shares acquired in the 9 days preceding a disposal on a first-in first-out basis.

(3) Shares comprised in a 'new holding'.

(4) Shares within a '1982 holding'.

One of the consequences of these changes is that the well-known practice of establishing losses by 'bed-and-breakfasting' shares is once again possible under the simple procedure of sale and repurchase on consecutive days.

Where a company in which you have a holding is taken over, and instead of receiving cash you exchange your shares for shares in the new company, no disposal takes place at that time. Your new holding is regarded as having been acquired at the same time and for the same price as the old one.

Building society share accounts

Deposits are made in building society share accounts to earn interest and not to realize either capital profits or losses. Nevertheless, a withdrawal from, or closure of, an account ranks as a disposal and gives rise to a claim to the indexation allowance. The resulting loss, which will be equivalent to this allowance, can be offset against other gains in the normal way.

Tax saver

Illustration

£10,000 was invested in a 3-year-term share account in June 1984. The indexation allowance due when the fixed term expired in June 1987 is

$$£10,000 \times 0.142 \qquad £1,420$$

The government has indicated that legislation will be introduced in this year's Finance Bill to deny claims to the indexation allowance on disposals from building society share accounts after 3 July 1987.

Chattels

Gains on the sales of chattels with an expected life of more than fifty years sold for less than £3,000 are exempt from tax. For items which fetch between £3,000 and £7,500 the chargeable gain is restricted to 5/3 times the amount of the proceeds of sale (ignoring expenses) over £3,000 where this is to the taxpayer's advantage.

Illustration

A piece of antique furniture purchased in 1972 for £830 was sold in August 1987 for £5,400. Although the profit on sale was £4,570 the chargeable gain, ignoring the indexation allowance, is restricted to £4,000, being 5/3 × (£5,400—£3,000).

Where an article is sold at a loss for under £3,000, the allowable loss is restricted by assuming the proceeds on sale were equivalent to £3,000.

Illustration

A painting was purchased many years ago for £6,320. It subsequently transpired that it was a fake and was sold for £90. The loss on sale, ignoring the indexation allowance, is restricted to £3,320, being £6,320 less £3,000.

Articles comprising a set are regarded as a single item when they are sold to the same person but at different times.

Wasting assets

Wasting assets are assets with an expected life span of less than fifty years. Unless it comes within the definition of 'tangible moveable property' a gain on the sale of a wasting asset is calculated in the same way as that on the sale of any other asset, except that the purchase price wastes away during the asset's expected life span. Leases of land for less than fifty years are wasting assets. A specific table is provided for calculating the proportion of the purchase of a lease which can be deducted from the sale proceeds.

The gain on a sale of a wasting asset which is also 'tangible moveable property' is exempt from tax. Neither does a loss on a sale of similar property count as an allowable loss.

Part disposals

Where you only sell part of an asset its acquisition cost is apportioned between the part sold and the proportion retained. This is done on a pro rata basis by reference to the proceeds of sale of the part sold and the open-market value of the proportion retained. The indexation allowance is calculated on the cost of the part sold. The proportion of the original cost of the asset attributable to the part which was not sold can be set against the proceeds on a sale of the remainder at a later date.

If the part sold is small compared to the value of the entire asset or shareholding you can claim to deduct the sale proceeds from the acquisition cost. Where the part disposal is one of land this procedure can be adopted so long as the sale proceeds are both less than £20,000 and one fifth of the value of the remaining land.

Business assets
If you are in business and dispose of an asset used in your trade you have to pay Capital Gains Tax on the profit of sale. The profit or loss is calculated in the same way as that on a disposal of an asset you own personally. If the proceeds of sale are reinvested wholly or partly in other assets for use in the business, payment of the tax on the profit can be wholly or partly postponed. This is achieved by reducing the cost of the replacement assets by the capital gain realized on the disposal of the old asset.

When you come to dispose of your business assets on retirement either by sale or gift the first £125,000 of capital gains is exempt from tax. To qualify automatically for this maximum exemption you must have been in business for at least ten years and be over age 60 at the time of the disposal. The age qualification applies equally to both sexes. You can only claim this relief before age 60 if you retire prematurely owing to ill health.

The precise rules which apply in calculating the capital gain on the disposal of a business asset during the course of trading or on retirement are complicated. It is outside the scope of this book to go into them in detail. The indexation allowance features in both of them.

Gifts
Where there is a capital gain on an asset you give away you can

elect with the transferee for payment of the tax to be postponed until the asset is subsequently disposed of by the transferee. The capital gain on the transfer is calculated by using the market value of the asset at the date of gift. The amount of the gain is reduced by the indexation allowance which is due at the time.

Inheritances
No Capital Gains tax is payable on the unrealized profits on your assets at the date of your death. When you inherit an asset you acquire it at the value on the date of death of the deceased. Generally, this rule is also applied whenever you become entitled to assets from a trust. As the trustees will usually be liable to Capital Gains Tax on the unrealized gains at the time of transfer, payment of the tax can be postponed in a similar way to that which applies on gifts. You have to join in with the trustees in making this election.

Assets held on 6 April 1965
Apart from quoted stocks and shares, a gain on the sale of an asset which you have owned since before 6 April 1965 is reduced. This is done to eliminate from the charge to tax the profit on sale attributable to the period up to 5 April 1965, the date when Capital Gains Tax was introduced. This reduction is achieved by assuming the gain was made evenly on a time basis throughout the period of ownership. The taxable part of the gain is determined as follows:

$$\frac{\text{Period of time from 6 April 1965 to the date of sale}}{\text{Period of time from acquisition to the date of sale}} \times \text{Overall gain}$$

Alternatively, it is possible for you to elect for the value of the asset on 6 April 1965 to be substituted in the calculation of the capital gain arising on sale. You will choose to make this election in writing to your tax office where your taxable gain comes out at a lower figure.

Illustration
A property purchased in May 1962 for £3,000 was sold in May 1987 for £50,000. On 6 April 1965 it had a value of £9,000. At 31 March 1982 it was

worth £25,000. The indexation allowance between March 1982 and May 1987 is 0.283.

The first calculation of the chargeable gain is:

	£	£
Sale proceeds		50,000
Less: Purchase price	3,000	
Indexation allowance		
£25,000 × 0.283	7,075	
		10,075
Gross gain		£39,925

Time apportionment:

$$\frac{\text{April 1965 to May 1987} = 265 \text{ months}}{\text{May 1962 to May 1987} = 300 \text{ months}} \times £39,925 = £35,267$$

The second calculation of the chargeable gain is:

	£	£
Sale proceeds		50,000
Less: 6 April 1965 value	9,000	
Indexation allowance		
£25,000 × 0.283	7,075	
		16,075
Chargeable gain		£33,925

It is to the taxpayer's advantage to make an election for the 6 April 1965 value to be used in calculating the capital gain.

Perhaps you still own some quoted investments which were purchased before 6 April 1965. You may already have elected for them to be regarded as if they had been bought on 6 April 1965 at their market value at that date. If this is so then any additions to, or part disposals of, these shareholdings up until 5 April 1982 were treated as a pool in the way described in an earlier section in this chapter. If no election has been made to use the 6 April 1965 value then the profit or loss on sale is found by comparing the sale proceeds with either the original cost of the investment or its value on 6 April 1965. The chargeable gain is the lower of the two figures. If one calculation results in a gain and the other throws up a loss, the transaction is treated as giving rise to neither gain nor loss.

11

COMPLETING THE RETURN

When you collect your post up from the doormat you can always pick out your Tax Return from the other letters. It comes in a distinctive brown envelope at the same time every year. Try to avoid the temptation to put it to one side. Although it might not prove possible to complete the Return and send it back to your tax office within the required thirty days, it is better to deal with it promptly. At least your tax office can then see that you are being given the correct allowances and reliefs in the code number which your employer is using to calculate the regular deductions for PAYE from your salary or wages. If your Return shows that you owe some additional tax on your income or you have realized some capital gains, the Inspector of Taxes will send you any assessments to collect the tax due. Failure to deal with your Tax Return quickly can often result in the Inland Revenue sending you assessments showing your income has been estimated. What you do when you receive one of these is dealt with in Chapter 12.

Not everyone is sent a Tax Return. If you do not receive one it is probably because your tax office think your only income is your salary or wage taxed under PAYE. If this is so and you are satisfied you are being given all the personal allowances and reliefs which you claim you need do nothing more. On the other hand, if you have received additional income which is taxable you should ask for a Tax Return so you can declare it to the Inland Revenue and pay any tax due on it. Failure to do this will lead to the imposition of both interest and penalties.

There are several different types of Income Tax Return. The following list shows which one you can expect to receive:

Form Number	Classification of Taxpayer
11	Standard full return for self-employed person
11P	Standard full return for employee
11K	Non-domiciled individual
11 (Lloyds)	Lloyds underwriter
P1	Simplified return for employee
R40	Taxpayer entitled to a repayment
R40(S)	Tax repayment claim for student
R232	Minors repayment claim

With your Tax Return comes a 'Tax Return Guide', which will help you complete the form, and a copy of the Taxpayer's Charter (see Chapter 1). A Tax Return form is reproduced in Chapter 15, filled out by a fictional character.

This book is being published at about the time you should be receiving your 1988/89 Tax Return. You may well ask why the Return refers to the tax year which has just started rather than the one which has just finished. The answer is that the form serves two purposes. It acts as a report of your income, outgoings and capital gains for the year ended on 5 April 1988, but the section on allowances is for the year to 5 April 1989.

As there is not a great deal of space in each section of the Return you can always provide more detailed information on a separate statement and only show the total income for a particular item on the form. When you do this every item on your Return for which there is a supporting statement should be noted 'see schedule attached' or words to that effect.

Let us now go through the sections in the form to understand what needs to be shown under the various headings and where you will be able to find this information. Remember if you are a married man you must also give full details of your wife's income, outgoings and capital gains. When the Return is finished it must be signed in the space provided on the back page. Bear in mind the wording of the Declaration: 'To the best of my knowledge and belief the particulars given on this form are correct and complete.'

Income

Form P60 — your certificate of pay and tax deducted — given to you by your employer shortly after the end of the tax year will tell you the amount of your salary or wages to enter on the Tax Return. You should keep this form so that if you receive a formal assessment on your earnings you can check the figure of tax deducted from them with that shown on the P60. If you are a company director or earn more than £8,500 per annum your employer will complete a Form P11D detailing your benefits-in-kind and other expenses payments. You should ask for a copy of this and enter your taxable benefits.

The amount of your pension from a previous employer's pension fund will also be notified to you on a Form P60. If either you or your wife are drawing the National Insurance Retirement Pension or some other benefit from the State you should declare the amount of your income for the 52-week period to 5 April 1988. Particularly where your National Insurance Pension is paid quarterly there will be a small difference between the income you should show on the Return and the actual pension received during the tax year. Some State benefits are exempt from tax.

If you are self-employed you will have to prepare a statement of the income and expenses from your business. You should do this along the lines set out in Chapter 5. On the Return Form you should enter the nature of your business and its address.

Your managing agents will have regularly sent you statements showing the rents receivable and expenses incurred for any properties which you let out. From these you should prepare a summary to accompany your Tax Return along the lines set out in Chapter 6.

The amount of interest earned during the year on your bank deposit account can be obtained from your bank statements. Most banks credit interest half-yearly at the end of each June and December. If you receive your interest at more regular intervals or had a large sum on deposit for short fixed periods you must make sure that the interest from all your accounts is reported on the Tax Return.

There is also a section in which to enter the amount of any building society interest received. You can normally obtain this information from your pass book. If you have an account which pays interest monthly you will need to enter the total of all your monthly receipts.

Dividends on your shareholdings come with counterfoils. These should always be kept. You can then list them and just enter on the Tax Return the total of all your dividends and tax credits during the tax year. The list should be sent in with the Tax Return. The same procedure should be followed where you are receiving fixed-interest payments from which tax is deducted at source.

If you are fortunate enough to be receiving income from a trust, the trustee will send you a certificate showing your income each year. You should enter the gross amount in the space provided in the Return.

There are other sections in the part of your Return dealing with your income but they are unlikely to be of general application.

Outgoings

This part of the Return is almost entirely devoted to your borrowings and the interest paid on these. The purposes for which you can take out a loan and get tax relief on the interest are set out in Chapter 3. Make sure you attach to the Tax Return any certificate of interest paid where this is relevant.

Use this part of the form to claim relief for any expenses, such as professional subscriptions, incurred in connection with your employment.

Details of all the covenants you have taken out need to be entered on the Return. You should include the gross amounts for all your covenanted payments including any charitable ones.

If you are making payments to a former or separated wife there is a space for these to be entered. This also applies to amounts you are paying to your children under a court order. Again, it is the gross amounts which need to be reported.

Capital gains

Every time you buy or sell shares or securities your broker sends you a contract note. Do not lose these as you will need them to complete this part of the Return. In order that any Capital Gains Tax due from you can be calculated, enter on the Return details of all the assets you sold during the tax year. Even if you think a profit on sale is exempt from tax, still report the sale in this section. Where your total chargeable gains, before losses, are less than £6,600 and the total proceeds of all your sales during the year are under £13,200 it will normally be sufficient to write in this section of the Return: 'gains not exceeding £6,600 and disposal proceeds not exceeding £13,200'.

Allowances

All the various personal allowances are set out in this part of the Return Form. In each case there is a space for you to enter the information the Inland Revenue need to tell whether you are entitled to be given the allowance. You will be well advised to look through each section carefully. I suggest you refer back to Chapter 2 which dealt with the various personal allowances and who can claim them.

Penalties

Earlier in this chapter I made a passing reference to the powers of the Inland Revenue to impose interest and penalties. This will happen if you omit to tell your tax office about some source of income or capital gain or fail to submit your Tax Returns promptly. Making an incomplete or incorrect Tax Return or statement is also a serious offence which will lead to the levy of a penalty. If you can show you had a reasonable excuse for failing to comply with your obligations as a taxpayer, and these are remedied without undue delay after they have been discovered, then no penalty should be imposed by the Inland Revenue. The maximum penalties which are prescribed are:

Offence	Penalty
Failure to notify liability to tax within one year after the end of the tax year in which it arises	£100
Failure to complete a Tax Return	£50, plus a possible extra £10 a day. Where the failure continues beyond the end of the tax year after that in which the Return was issued the penalty is increased to £50 plus the tax payable based on the Return.
Making an incorrect Return or statement	£50, plus the amount of tax lost by the Inland Revenue. In the case of fraud the penalty is increased to twice the amount of tax lost.

The Inland Revenue will usually charge a penalty below the maximum limit. This depends on the seriousness of the offence and other circumstances. In addition to charging a penalty the Inland Revenue will also claim interest. This will be calculated from the date when the tax was normally due. These dates are set out in Chapter 12.

12

ASSESSMENTS AND REPAYMENT CLAIMS

If you ignore an assessment of demand sent to you by the Inland Revenue, the end result can come as an unpleasant surprise. Your responsibilities as a taxpayer are not just confined to completing your Tax Return each year. It is also important you understand what action you need to take whenever you receive an assessment and how to claim any repayment due to you.

Appeals

Each assessment sent to you will tell you how long you have in which to appeal against it. This time limit is usually thirty days. If you are late in dealing with the Return you run the risk of assessments being sent to you by the Inland Revenue which require some action within this appeal period. Providing you complete your Tax return promptly it is less likely that any assessments you receive will be inaccurate.

The Inland Revenue have a special Form 64-7 for giving an appeal against an assessment. One of these forms will usually be sent to you with each assessment. You are not bound to use it: if you prefer to make your objection in a letter this will do. What is important is that your appeal should clearly state the reasons why you disagree with the assessment. This will usually be because the Inland Revenue have estimated your income or business profits in the absence of your Tax return or accounts. Where the assessment is excessive you should say so in your appeal. Alternatively, if it is not in accordance with information already sent, or to be provided, to the Inland Revenue then this will be the basis of your appeal. Wherever possible try and send the Inland Revenue the missing Return or outstanding information as soon as you can.

Inevitably the incorrect assessment shows you owe some tax. Where you think this is more than the amount which will ultimately be payable you should request that collection of the excess be postponed. Do this at the same time as your appeal. You must specify your reasons why you want all or part of the tax charged on the assessment postponed. Unless an application for postponement is made all the tax will be due and payable on the date shown on the assessment.

The majority of appeals are eventually settled by agreement between the taxpayer and the Inland Revenue. The assessment will then be adjusted to the agreed figures. There are occasions when agreement cannot be reached. The procedure for resolving your appeal starts with a hearing before the General Tax Commissioners. It can then move on to the Courts and ultimately to the House of Lords.

Should you ever reach the stage of receiving notification of a hearing of an appeal before the General Commissioners you ignore it at your peril. This is because the Commissioners have the power to determine your appeal. Unless you are represented at the hearing you can end up paying more than the true amount of tax due on the assessment.

Normal dates for tax payments
For the tax year 1987/88 these are:

Type of Assessment	Date of payment
Income Tax and Class 4 National Insurance contributions on business profits	Half on 1 January 1988, half on 1 July 1988
Income Tax on rents and untaxed interests	1 January 1988
Higher rate tax and investment income surcharge on taxed investment income	1 December 1988
Capital gains tax	1 December 1988

Interest on overdue tax
If you delay paying your tax after it is due you face the prospect of being charged interest. The current rate is 8.25% per annum. The interest is calculated from the due date up until payment.

Except where an appeal is given against an assessment the due date will either be one of those in the preceding section in this chapter or thirty days after the assessment is issued if that is later. Where the interest is less than £30 it will not normally be collected.

Repayment claims

There are a number of situations which can lead to a tax refund. This can simply arise because you have paid more tax than you should have done. Alternatively, perhaps your business had a bad year and made a loss. A repayment would be due to you by setting the loss against other income on which tax had already been paid. In these situations the Inland Revenue will send your refund as soon as they receive a request for repayment from you.

There are also those taxpayers whose income mainly comes from investments. When they come to claim their personal allowances they will usually end up receiving an income tax repayment.

Illustration

A single woman had an income from dividends of £2,044 net during 1987/88. She also received building society interest of £1,752, and her earnings from a part-time employment were £1,200.

	Income £	Tax deducted £
Casual earnings	1,200	
Dividends	2,800	756.00
Building society interest	2,400	648.00
	6,400	1,404.00
Less: Personal allowance	2,425	
Taxable income	£3,975	
Tax thereon:		
£3,975 at 27%		1,073.25
1987/88 repayment		£330.75

Repayment supplement

Whenever the Inland Revenue refund more than £25 they have

to work out whether to supplement it by a payment of interest. The current rate is 8.25% per annum and the supplement is not taxable. It is calculated from one of two dates, whichever is the later. The first is the end of the tax year following the one for which the repayment is due. The second is the end of the year of assessment in which the tax was paid.

Remission of tax

There are occasions when the Inland Revenue do not act promptly after they receive your Tax Return or other information about a change in your circumstances. Where there is no response from the tax office it is not unreasonable for you to believe that your affairs are in order. If you were subsequently faced with a large demand which had built up through this sort of oversight it could cause you considerable hardship.

Tax saver

In recognition of this the Inland Revenue will not collect all the arrears of tax which have built up because of a failure to make proper and timely use of information supplied by the taxpayer. The amount you are let off depends on the size of your income when you are notified of the arrears. At present the following table applies:

Gross Income			
Under 65	Over 65	Remit	Collect
up to £8,500	up to £11,000	All	None
£8,501 to £10,500	£11,001 to £13,000	75%	25%
£10,501 to £13,500	£13,001 to £16,000	50%	50%
£13,501 to £16,000	£16,001 to £18,500	25%	75%
£16,001 to £23,000	£18,501 to £25,500	10%	90%

13

ELECTIONS AND CLAIMS — TIME LIMITS

You will already have gathered that certain options available to you as a taxpayer are dependent on you submitting an election or claim to the Inspector of Taxes. As these will usually involve a saving in tax it is important to appreciate that all elections or claims must be submitted within prescribed time limits. This chapter brings together those elections and claims which are most likely to concern you. It also sets out the time available during which they must be submitted to the Inspector of Taxes. It is by no means exhaustive.

Election/Claim	Time Limit
Chapter 2 — Personal Allowances and Reliefs	
Claim to the various personal allowances detailed in the chapter	Six years after the year of assessment
Chapter 5 — The Self-Employed	
Claim for the second and third years of assessment of a new business to be revised to the actual profits earned in those years	Seven years after the end of the second year of assessment
Relief for losses sustained in the year of assessment	Two years after the year of assessment in which the loss is made
Relief for the loss sustained in the preceding year of assessment	Three years after the year of assessment in which the loss is made
Relief for the loss in the first four years of assessment of a new business to be given against the income of the three preceding years of assessment	Two years after the year of assessment in which the loss occurred

Retirement-annuity premiums to be treated as paid in the preceding year of assessment	5 April in the year of assessment in which payment was made

Chapter 6 — Investment Income

Claim for the third year of assessment on a source of untaxed interest to be adjusted to the actual interest earned in the year	Six years after the year of assessment
Claim for relief under the Business Expansion Scheme	Two years after the end of the year of assessment in which the shares were issued or, if later, 28 months after the company begins to trade
Election requiring your woodlands to be taxed as if it were a business	Two years after the end of the chargeable period

Chapter 7 — The Family Unit

Election for separate assessment of Income Tax or revocation of such an election	Within six months before 6 July in the year of assessment
Election for the separation taxation of wife's earnings or revocation of such an election	Not earlier than six months before the beginning or later than twelve months after the year of assessment
Disclaimer by husband of Income Tax and/or Capital Gains Tax on wife's death	Within two months of the date of grant of probate or of letters of administration (or later if the wife's executors agree)

Chapter 10 — Capital Gains Tax

Claim for the indexation allowance to be calculated on the market value of an asset at 31 March 1982	Two years after the year of assessment in which the disposal occurs. By concession a claim can be withdrawn within this two-year period if the Capital Gains Tax assessment is not final
Election for separate assessment of Capital Gains Tax or revocation of such an election	By 6 July following the year of assessment

Claim to the capital loss where the value of an asset becomes negligible	The loss arises on the date of claim although, in practice, a two-year period is allowed from the time the asset became of negligible value
Claim for the loss on shares that were originally subscribed for in an unquoted trading company to be set against income in the year of loss, or the following year	Two years after the year of assessment in which the relief is taken
An election to determine which of your homes is to be regarded as your principle private residence for Capital Gains Tax purposes	Two years from the date when two or more properties are eligible
Claim to exemption from Capital Gains Tax on the disposal of a residence occupied by a dependent relative	Six years from the year in which the gain arose
Election to pool quoted securities held at 6 April 1965	Two years from the period in which the first relevant disposal occurred
Claim to roll-over relief on the disposal of business assets	Six years after the year of assessment
Claim for the 6 April 1965 value to be substituted in a calculation of the capital gain arising on the sale of an asset held at that date	Two years from the year of assessment in which the disposal is made

14

INHERITANCE TAX

Inheritance Tax was introduced by the Chancellor in 1986 as the successor to Capital Transfer Tax. Some of the features of the new tax are similar to the Estate Duty rules which applied before Capital Transfer Tax was introduced back in 1974. Not only might it be payable on transfers or gifts you make during your lifetime, but it is also due on the value of your estate on death. Unlike the rules which apply for Income Tax, husband and wife are treated as separate individuals. Both are entitled to the various exemptions. Inheritance Tax is far from straightforward. What follows is a brief outline. The Tax is administered by the Capital Taxes Office, to whom any Returns should be submitted.

Potentially exempt transfers

The most significant feature of the new Inheritance Tax is the concept of a potentially exempt transfer (PET). This is:

(1) An outright gift to an individual.
(2) A gift into an accumulation-and-maintenance settlement.
(3) A gift into a settlement for the benefit of a disabled person.
(4) A gift into an interest in possession trust.
(5) The termination of an interest in possession settlement where the settled property passes to an individual, an accumulation and maintenance settlement, or a trust for the benefit of a disabled person.

No tax is payable providing the donor lives for at least seven years after making the gift. A form of tapering relief applies where death occurs within seven years. The amount of Inheritance Tax is then calculated at the rates which apply at the date of death as shown in the following table:

Number of Years Between Gift and death	% of Tax Payable
Not more than 3	100
Between 3 and 4	80
Between 4 and 5	60
Between 5 and 6	40
Between 6 and 7	20

Gifts with reservation

If you make a gift but continue to enjoy some benefit from it, the property or asset you have given away is likely to be treated as yours until either the date when you cease to enjoy any benefit from the gift or your death. This is a 'gift with reservation'. For example, you give your house to your children but continue to live there, rent free. Your house would then be counted as part of your estate at the time of your death.

Lifetime gifts

If you make a gift during your lifetime which is not a potentially exempt transfer it will attract liability to Inheritance Tax at one half of the rates which apply on death. An example of such a lifetime gift is a transfer into a discretionary trust.

Exemptions

The main exemptions applicable to individuals are:

(1) Transfers between husband and wife.

(2) Gifts up to £3,000 in any one tax year. Any part of the exemption which is left over can be carried forward to the following year only. For example, if your total transfers came to £1,500 during 1986/87 you could have given away as much as £4,500 during 1987/88 all within your annual exemption limit.

(3) Gifts to any one person up to £250 per person in each tax year. Where the total amount given to any one individual exceeds this limit no part comes within this exemption.

(4) Marriage gifts. The amount you can give away depends on your relationship to the bride or bridegroom, as follows:

	£
By either parent	5,000
By a grandparent or great grandparent	2,500
By bridegroom to bride or vice versa	2,500
By any other person	1,000

(5) Regular gifts out of income which form part of your normal expenditure.

(6) Gifts and bequests to charities without limit.

(7) Gifts to political parties (limited to £100,000 where these are on, or within one year of, death).

Rates of tax

Each taxable gift or transfer is not considered in isolation in calculating how much tax is payable on it. In working out how much is payable, previous taxable transfers are taken into account. This is because the tax due on each chargeable gift or the value of your estate on death is dependent upon the cumulative value of all other chargeable transfers in the seven years leading up to the date of the next chargeable transfer. The rates payable on death from 17 March 1987 are:

Band	Rate	Tax on Band	Cumulative Tax
£	%	£	£
0— 90,000	0	Nil	Nil
90,001—140,000	30	15,000	15,000
140,001—220,000	40	32,000	47,000
220,001—330,000	50	55,000	102,000
Over 330,000	60		

These rates also apply to all lifetime gifts or transfers within three years of death. Inheritance Tax payable on PETS more than three years before but within seven years of death is determined by the first table in this chapter.

Like the main personal Income Tax allowances, both the limit of £90,000 on chargeable transfers taxable at a nil rate and the other rate bands go up each year. The increase is measured by the movement in the Retail Prices Index during the previous calendar year. A rounding-up adjustment may be necessary.

Miscellaneous aspects

Business assets, including shares you own in a family company, along with agricultural property and woodlands, qualify for special relief for Inheritance Tax purposes. The Tax can also apply in varying ways to different types of trust.

15

THE TAX AFFAIRS OF DAVID JONES —
A CASE STUDY

The story

This is the story of David Jones and his family. David retired
two years ago — on his 65th birthday. He receives a pension
from his former employer's pension scheme as well as the
basic National Insurance Retirement Pension. He is still paying
off a small mortgage of around £5,000 on the house where he
lives with his wife Sarah.

Sarah is ten years younger than David. She works as a
designer for a local firm. Her employers provide her with a
company car, all expenses paid, and pay into a private-health-
care insurance policy for her. She pays an annual subscription
to the Institute of Designers. As the firm has no company
pension scheme, Sarah pays regularly each year into her own
personal pension plan.

Throughout his working life David always managed to put
aside some of his earnings for the day when he retired. He has a
National Savings Bank Investment Account as well as a small
portfolio of shares, unit trusts and government stocks. He
keeps his spare cash in a bank deposit account. Sarah favours
the local building society as the home for her savings.

David has taken out deeds of covenant in favour of both the
local parish church and his granddaughter Samantha.

Tragically David's parents were both killed in a car accident
20 years ago. As he was an only child they left him all their pos-
sessions. One of these was a picture which David sold at auc-
tion last June. It fetched £30,000 net of expenses. Back in 1967

when his parents died it was only worth £4,000. In March 1982 it would have sold for £20,000. Last July David also sold one of his shareholdings for £5,000. The shares cost him £2,000 in May 1983. He has reinvested the proceeds of these two sales in his National Savings Bank Investment Account.

David's 1988/89 Tax Return
This is reproduced on the following eight pages.

David's tax liabilities for 1987/88
(1) Under PAYE

	£	£
Pensions — State	2,054	
— Fieldgate Publishing Company Ltd.	3,000	
		5,054
Wife's salary	20,000	
Wife's taxable benefits	1,700	
		21,700
		26,754
Less: Subscription	31	
Pension premium	1,000	
Personal allowance	3,795	
Wife's earned income relief	2,425	
		7,251
Taxable Income		£19,503
Tax thereon:		
First £18,700 @ 27%		5,049.00
Next £803 @ 40%		321.20
Tax deductible under PAYE for 1987/88		£5,370.20

Notes:

(a) As David and Sarah's mortgage is under MIRAS (see Chapter 3) the actual amount of interest paid to the building society during the year was:

(continued on page 112)

SPECIMEN FORM

**Inland Revenue
Tax Return 1988-89**

Income, Class 4 National Insurance contributions
and Capital Gains for year ended 5 April 1988

Allowances for year ending 5 April 1989

H.M. Inspector of Taxes	Date of issue	Reference	National Insurance no.
A. N. Other	6th April 1988	195/F249	FX 57 30 29 C

Fieldgate District
Fieldgate House,
Fieldgate
TA6 7DP

Mr. D. Jones,
79 Acorn Street,
Fieldgate,
TA6 2RY

You are required to complete pages 2-8 of this form, sign the Declaration on page 8 and send it back to me within 30 days.
It will help if you will also give the information requested below.

*Please read the introduction to the enclosed notes before you start to fill in the form; the notes are there to help you.
Please ask me if you need any further help or information. If you find that there is insufficient room in any section,
please attach a separate sheet.*

Pensions information these details will help me to give you the right PAYE code

If you or your wife receive a pension, please give the following details —

Type of pension	Say if it is paid weekly, 4 weekly, monthly or quarterly ➜	Amount(s) you receive Self	Wife
FIELDGATE PUBLISHING Co. LTD.	MONTHLY	250.00	
NATIONAL INSURANCE RETIREMENT PENSION	4 WEEKLY	164.60	

If you or your wife are likely to start receiving a pension before 6 April 1989, please
give the following details —

Starting date	Type of pension	Say if it is payable weekly, 4 weekly, monthly or quarterly ➜	Amount(s) you will receive Self	Wife

If you or your wife were born before
6 April 1929, please give date(s) of birth: ▶ Self 26-03-1921 Wife

11P (1988)   1

SPECIMEN FORM

See note			Self	Wife
	Income: 6 April 1987 to 5 April 1988			
1-3	**Employment, etc.**			
	Earnings (including fees, bonus, commission, etc) from duties performed wholly in the UK			
	Occupation and employers name(s) and addresses)		£	£
	DESIGNER : FIELDGATE TEXTILE Co. LTD. FLOWERS LANE FIELDGATE TA6 5NZ			20,000
4-5	Benefits/expense allowances		Self	Wife
			£	£
	CAR BENEFIT			700
	CAR FUEL BENEFIT			600
	MEDICAL INSURANCE			400
	Tips	*Details*	£	£
6	Leaving payments and compensation	*Details*	£	£
7	If you or your wife received a taxed sum from the trustees of an approved profit sharing scheme, enter an "X" here		Self ☐	Wife ☐
	If the sum is included in the income shown above, enter an "X" here		☐	☐
8	Earnings from duties performed wholly or partly abroad		Self	Wife
	Employment concerned		£	£
	Dates absent from UK when working abroad. *Enclose statement if necessary.*		To claim dedn enter "X" ☐	☐
11	**Social Security pensions and Benefits**		Self	Wife
12	Retirement or old person's pension. If wife's pension (or part of it) is paid by virtue of her own contributions' enter an "X" here ► ☐		2054	£
13	Unemployment or Supplementary benefits *enter the full taxable amount*		£	£
	Widows and other benefits - *say what type (from order book)*		£	£
14-15	**Pension from former employer and other pensions**		Self	Wife
	Name and address of payers)		£	£
	FIELDGATE PUBLISHING Co. LTD., BUSH RD, FIELDGATE, TA6 3DY		3000	

2

SPECIMEN FORM

See note				Self	Wife
	Income: 6 April 1987 to 5 April 1988				

Trade, profession or vocation

See note				Self	Wife
17-19	Business name and address	Type of income		£	£
		Enterprise allowance		£	£
20		Balancing charges		£	£
		Deductions for Capital Allowances		£	£
21	Deduction for Class 4 National Insurance Contributions enter 'X' here			▶	

If your profits for Class 4 National Insurance Contributions purposes are affected by interest paid, certain capital allowances or losses not given in the assessment, give details on a separate sheet and enter 'X' here ▶

Property in the UK

See note	*delete as appropriate	Address	Gross income including premiums	Expenses (enclose statement)	Self	Wife
25	*Unfurnished lettings		£	£		
	*Furnished lettings					
	*Furnished holiday lettings					
26	*Ground rents or					
27	Feu duties					
	*Land					

UK Interest not taxed before receipt
Enter ALL the interest on each account or holding

See note				Self	Wife
	Enter interest taxed before receipt on page 4	National Savings	NSB Ordinary account ▶	£	£
29			NSB Investment account ▶	£ 1800	£
			Deposit or Income Bonds ▶	£	£
30	Other banks in the UK				
	Name of bank			£	£
31	Other UK sources (including War Loan, British Savings Bonds and loans to private individuals)				
	Description of source			£	£

Untaxed income from abroad

See note		Self	Wife
32	Details	£	£

3

SPECIMEN FORM

Income: 6 April 1987 to 5 April 1988

33

Interest treated as taxed before receipt (Composite Rate Tax)

Interest from UK banks and deposit takers taxed before receipt

Name of bank or deposit taker	Self £	Wife £
FIELDGATE BANK plc.	146	

33

Interest from UK building societies

Name of society	£	£
FIELDGATE BUILDING SOCIETY		365

36

Dividends from UK companies and tax credits

Name of UK company	Amount of dividend £	Amount of tax credit £
Self SHARES AND UNIT TRUST HOLDINGS — As SEPARATE STATEMENT	219	81
Wife		

37-40

Other dividends, trust income, etc, already taxed

Name of source (show each separately)	Gross amount of income
Self GOVERNMENT STOCKS — AS SEPARATE STATEMENT	400
Wife	£

41

Settlements Include income and capital from settlements, parental gifts, etc. and transfers to be treated as your income

	Self £	Wife £

4

SPECIMEN FORM

See note				Self	Wife

Income: 6 April 1987 to 5 April 1988

42 **Payments from estates** *Include receipts from the estates of deceased persons in Administration*

	Self	Wife
	£	£

43-51 **All other profits or income** *enter gross amounts*

Maintenance, alimony, or aliment received

	Self	Wife
	£	£

Any other income not entered elsewhere eg: *accrued income charges and taxable gains on life assurance policies*

	Self	Wife
	£	£

Outgoings: 6 April 1987 to 5 April 1988

Expenses in employment

		Self	Wife
56	Details of expenses	£	£
57	Fees or subscriptions to professional bodies *Name of professional body* INSTITUTE OF DESIGNERS	£	£ 31

94 **Payroll giving**

If any of these deductions or exemptions have been made from your or your wife's pay, enter an 'X' here ▶

Superannuation	Payments to charity	Profit Related Pay scheme
☐	☐	☐

Interest on loans for the purchase or improvement of property in the UK
Do not include bank overdrafts

Loans for only or main residence

58-60 Building society loan at 5/4/88 *Do not put amounts*

Name of society FIELDGATE BUILDING SOCIETY	*Account number* J 23615	Please tick box if you did not pay under the net interest arrangements (MIRAS) ▶ ☐

Building society loan paid off in year to 5/4/88 *Do not put amounts*

Name of society	*Account number*	Please tick box if you did not pay under the net interest arrangements (MIRAS) ▶ ☐

All other lenders *Include amounts*

Name(s) of lender(s)	*Account number(s)*	Self £	Wife £

If all interest is paid net to a lender other than a Building Society, enclose an interest certificate **only** where you claim tax relief for rates higher than basic rate. Always enclose an interest certificate if you paid any interest outside the MIRAS arrangements.

5

SPECIMEN FORM

Outgoings: 6 April 1987 to 5 April 1988

Interest on loans for the purchase or improvement of property in the UK continued
Do not include bank overdrafts

61 — Let property (other than furnished holiday lets)

Address *enclose certificate*	Number of weeks let	Self £	Wife £

58,62 — **Interest on other loans** *enclose certificates*

Name of lender	Self £	Wife £

Other outgoings
enter gross amounts before deduction of tax
Covenants, bonds of annuity, settlements, covenanted payments to charities, accrued income purchased etc.

63,66 67

Details		Self	Wife
COVENANTS:	FIELDGATE PARISH CHURCH	£ 200	£
	SAMANTHA JONES	500	

64 — Alimony, aliment or maintenance paid

Details	Self £	Wife £

65 — UK property rents or yearly interest paid to persons abroad

Details	Self £	Wife £

68 — Changes in untaxed income or outgoings since 5 April 1987

Details

Capital Gains: 6 April 1987 to 5 April 1988

70-80 — **Chargeable assets disposed of**

Amount of gain for year

Date of disposal	Description	Self £	Wife £
JUNE AND JULY 1987	AS ENCLOSED COMPUTATIONS	22934	

6

SPECIMEN FORM

See note

Allowances: Claim for year 6 April 1988 to 5 April 1989
Before making any claim, please read the appropriate note. Tick the box which applies and give the information asked for

83 ✓ **Married man's allowance** To claim this you must be living with or wholly maintaining your wife

Wife's first name(s)   SARAH LOUISE

If you were married after 5 April 1987, give — **both** | Date of marriage | **and** | Wife's former surname

84 ✓ **Age allowance** To claim this you or your wife must have been born before 6 April 1924

85 ☐ **Additional personal allowance**

Child's name (Surname first)

Child's date of birth

If the child was 16 or over on 6 April 1988 and receiving full time education or training, give the name of the university, college, school or type of training

Does he or she live with you?   Yes ☐   No ☐

Is any other person claiming the allowance for the child?   Yes ☐   No ☐

If you are claiming because your wife is unable to look after herself, what is her illness or disability?

Is she likely to be unable to look after herself throughout the year ending 5 April 1989?   Yes ☐   No ☐

86 ☐ **Dependent relative allowance**

Dependant's name

Dependant's date of birth

Does he or she live with you?   Yes ☐   No ☐

What is the dependant's relationship to you or your wife (if mother, say if widowed, divorced or separated)?

What is the dependant's illness or disability (if any)?

What is the dependant's annual income (excluding voluntary contributions) from:

State pension or benefit   £

Other pension   £

Other income   £

If the dependant does not live with you, enter the weekly amount you contribute   £

If any other relative contributes, enter the weekly amount contributed   £

87 ☐ **Blind person's allowance**
Local Authority or equivalent body with which registered and the date of registration — *say if self or wife*

93 ☐ **Personal pension plans**   If you pay contributions to a personal pension scheme or receive tax relief at source for contributions you pay to a scheme separate from your employer's pension scheme, enter an "X" here ▶ ☐

7

SPECIMEN FORM

See note

Allowances: Claim for year 6 April 1988 to 5 April 1989

88

☑ **Retirement annuity payments**

Enter the nature of your trade, profession or employment **unless** your earnings come from a non-pensionable employment where you should give the name of your employer.

Contract or scheme membership number

SF 421/35

FIELDGATE TEXTILE Co. LTD.

Amount paid in the year to 5 April 1988 £ 1000

Name of Insurance Company, etc or trust scheme

FIELDGATE INSURANCE Co.

Amount to be paid in the year to 5 April 1989 £ 1000

Enter your date of birth 04-09-1931

If you require a special form, enter an 'X' here ▶

92

☐ **Life assurance-limits to relief**

If in the year ended 5 April 1988 you and/or your wife paid more than —

£1275 in life assurance premiums (including deferred annuity premiums) enter the total paid £

£85 in deferred annuity premiums and compulsory payments to provide annuities for widows and orphans enter the total paid £

89-91

To claim any of the following allowances, tick the box that applies and I will send you the appropriate claim form.

☐ Son or daughter whose services you depend on

☐ Housekeeper allowance

☐ Friendly Society and Trade Union Death and Superannuation benefits

Declaration

False statements can result in prosecution

To the best of my knowledge and belief, the particulars given on this form are correct and complete

A woman should state after her signature whether she is single, married, widowed, separated or divorced

Signature *David Jones*.

Date 21 MAY 1988

If you are making the return as executor, trustee, receiver, factor, etc give the capacity in which you act and for whom the return is made.

Private address use CAPITAL letters

79 ACORN ST.
FIELDGATE

Postcode TA6 2RY

Please enter your National Insurance number if it is not already shown on the front of this form

If there is any other information which you think may affect your income tax liability, please give details on a separate piece of paper.

© Crown copyright 1987

	£
Gross interest	600
Less: Tax at the basic rate	162
Net Payment	£438

(b) The band of income up to £17,900 taxable at the basic rate has then to be extended by both the gross building society interest and the charitable covenant in favour of the local parish church, as follows:

	£
Income taxable at the basic rate	17,900
Gross building society interest	600
Gross covenanted payment	200
	£18,700

(2) Under Schedule D

Interest on National Savings Bank Investment Account	£500

Tax thereon at 40% payable on 1 January 1988	£200

Note:
David pays tax during 1987/88 on the interest earned during the previous tax year — 1986/87 (see Chapter 6).

(3) Higher rates on taxed income

	Gross Income
	£
Dividends and tax credits	300
Government stocks	400
Building society interest	500
Bank deposit interest	200
	£1,400

Tax thereon:

First £1,197 @ 40%		478.80
Next £203 @ 45%		91.35
		£570.15
Less: Tax deducted at source		378.00
Tax payable on 1 December 1988		£192.15

(4) Capital Gains Tax

		£
(a) Sale proceeds of picture		30,000
Less: Acquisition value	4,000	
Indexation allowance based on March 1982 value: £20,000 × 0.283	5,660	
		9,660
Chargeable gain		£20,340

		£
(b) Sale proceeds of shares		5,000
Less: Cost price	2,000	
Indexation allowance: £2,000 × 0.203	406	
		2,406
Chargeable gain		£2,594

Total chargeable gains	£22,934

Tax thereon:

First £6,600	Exempt
Next £16,334 @ 30%	4,900.20
Tax payable on 1 December 1988	£4,900.20

Note:

The increase in the Retail Price Index between March 1982 and June 1987 was 28.3%, and between May 1983 and July 1987 it amounted to 20.3%.

TABLE 1

Booklet No.	Title
IR 1	Extra Statutory Concessions
IR 4	Income Tax and Pensioners
IR 4A	Income Tax — Age Allowance
IR 11	Tax Treatment of Interest Paid
IR 13	Wife's Earnings Election
IR 20	Residents and Non-Residents Liability to Tax in the United Kingdom
IR 22	Income Tax — Personal Allowances
IR 23	Income Tax and Widows
IR 25	The Taxation of Foreign Earnings and Pensions
IR 27	Notes on the Taxation of Income From Real Property
IR 28	Starting in Business
IR 29	Income Tax and One-Parent Families
IR 30	Separation and Divorce
IR 31	Income Tax and Married Couples
IR 32	Separate Assessment
IR 33	Income Tax and School Leavers
IR 34	PAYE
IR 37	Income Tax and Capital Gains Tax: Appeals
IR 41	Income Tax and the Unemployed
IR 42	Income Tax: Lay-Offs and Short-Time Work
IR 43	Income Tax and Strikes
IR 45	Income Tax and Capital Gains: What Happens When Someone Dies
IR 47	An Income Tax Form Entitled Deed of Covenant by Parent to Adult Student
IR 51	Business Expansion Scheme
IR 52	Your Tax Office
IR 55	Bank Interest — Paying Tax
IR 56	Tax — Employed or Self-Employed?
IR 57	Thinking of Working for Yourself?
IR 59	Students' Tax Information Pack

TABLE 2

FLAT RATE ALLOWANCES FOR SPECIAL
CLOTHING AND THE UPKEEP OF TOOLS

(1) Fixed rate for all occupations

	£
Agricultural	45
Forestry	45
Quarrying	45
Brass and copper	65
Precious metals	45
Textile prints	40
Food	25
Glass	40
Railways	40
Uniformed prison officers	35
Uniformed bank employees	25
Uniformed police officers up to and including chief inspector	35

(2) Variable rate depending on category of occupation

Seamen	55/85/110
Iron mining	50/65
Iron and steel	30/40/80
Aluminium	30/40/65/85
Engineering	30/40/65/80
Shipyards	30/40/50/75
Vehicles	25/40/70
Particular engineering	30/40/65/80
Constructional engineering	30/40/50/75
Electrical and electrical supply	15/60
Textiles	40/55
Clothing	20/30
Leather	25/35
Printing	20/45/70
Building materials	25/35/55
Wood and furniture	30/50/60/75
Building	25/35/55/75
Heating	45/60/70
Public service	25/35

Note
The allowances are only available to manual workers who have to
bear the cost of upkeep of tools and special clothing. Other
employees, such as office staff, cannot claim them.

TABLE 3

RATES OF NATIONAL INSURANCE CONTRIBUTIONS FOR 1987/88

CLASS 1 contributions for employees

		Standard rate	Contracted-out On first £39.00	On remainder
Contributions levied on all weekly earnings if they reach but do not exceed	£39.00 £64.99	5%	5%	2.85%
All weekly earnings if they reach but do not exceed	£65.00 £99.99	7%	7%	4.85%
All weekly earnings if they reach but do not exceed	£100.00 £295.00	9%	9%	6.85%
If weekly earnings exceed	£295.00	No additional contributions	No additional contributions	

Reduced rate for married women and widows with a valid election certificate	3.85%
Men over 65 and women over 60	Nil
Lower earnings limit — weekly — monthly — annually	£39.00 £169.00 £2,028.00
Upper earnings limit — weekly — monthly — annually	£295.00 £1,279.00 £15,340.00

CLASS 2 contributions for the self-employed

Weekly flat rate	£3.85
Small earnings exception	£2,125.00

CLASS 3 voluntary contributions

Weekly rate	£3.75

CLASS 4 contributions for the self-employed

6.3% of profits between £4,590 and £15,340

TABLE 4

CAPITAL GAINS TAX – THE INDEXATION ALLOWANCE

Starting month for indexation	Month of Disposal 1987								
	Apr	May	Jun	Jul	Aug	Sept	Oct	Nov	Dec
1982									
Mar	.281	.283	.283	.281	.285	.289	.295	.302	.300
Apr	.256	.257	.257	.256	.260	.264	.270	.276	.275
May	.247	.248	.248	.247	.251	.255	.261	.267	.266
Jun	.244	.245	.245	.244	.247	.251	.257	.263	.262
Jul	.243	.245	.245	.243	.247	.251	.257	.263	.262
Aug	.243	.244	.244	.243	.247	.250	.256	.262	.261
Sept	.244	.245	.245	.244	.247	.251	.257	.263	.262
Oct	.238	.239	.239	.238	.241	.245	.251	.257	.256
Nov	.232	.233	.233	.232	.235	.239	.245	.251	.250
Dec	.234	.235	.235	.234	.237	.241	.247	.253	.252
1983									
Jan	.232	.233	.233	.232	.236	.240	.246	.252	.250
Feb	.227	.228	.228	.227	.231	.234	.240	.246	.245
Mar	.225	.226	.226	.225	.228	.232	.238	.244	.243
Apr	.208	.209	.209	.208	.211	.215	.221	.227	.226
May	.203	.204	.204	.203	.206	.210	.216	.222	.220
Jun	.200	.201	.201	.200	.203	.207	.213	.219	.218
Jul	.193	.195	.195	.193	.197	.200	.206	.212	.211
Aug	.188	.189	.189	.188	.192	.195	.201	.207	.206
Sept	.183	.184	.184	.183	.186	.190	.196	.202	.200
Oct	.179	.180	.180	.179	.182	.186	.191	.197	.196
Nov	.175	.176	.176	.175	.178	.182	.187	.193	.192
Dec	.172	.173	.173	.172	.175	.178	.184	.190	.189
1984									
Jan	.172	.173	.173	.172	.176	.179	.185	.191	.189
Feb	.167	.169	.169	.167	.171	.174	.180	.186	.185
Mar	.164	.165	.165	.164	.167	.171	.176	.182	.181
Apr	.148	.150	.150	.148	.152	.155	.161	.166	.165
May	.144	.145	.145	.144	.148	.151	.157	.162	.161
Jun	.141	.142	.142	.141	.145	.148	.154	.159	.158
Jul	.143	.144	.144	.143	.146	.149	.155	.160	.159
Aug	.132	.133	.133	.132	.135	.139	.144	.150	.149
Sept	.130	.131	.131	.130	.133	.136	.142	.147	.146
Oct	.123	.124	.124	.123	.126	.129	.135	.140	.139
Nov	.119	.120	.120	.119	.123	.126	.131	.137	.136
Dec	.120	.121	.121	.120	.124	.127	.132	.138	.137
1985									
Jan	.116	.117	.117	.116	.119	.123	.128	.134	.133
Feb	.107	.108	.108	.107	.111	.114	.119	.125	.124
Mar	.097	.098	.098	.097	.100	.103	.109	.114	.113
Apr	.074	.075	.075	.074	.077	.080	.086	.091	.090
May	.069	.070	.070	.069	.072	.076	.081	.086	.085
Jun	.067	.068	.068	.067	.070	.073	.078	.084	.083
Jul	.069	.070	.070	.069	.072	.075	.080	.086	.085
Aug	.066	.067	.067	.066	.069	.072	.078	.083	.082
Sept	.067	.068	.068	.067	.070	.073	.078	.083	.082
Oct	.065	.066	.066	.065	.068	.071	.076	.082	.081
Nov	.061	.062	.062	.061	.064	.068	.073	.078	.077
Dec	.060	.061	.061	.060	.063	.066	.071	.077	.076

1988 BUDGET HIGHLIGHTS

In what will probably be the last untelevised Budget Speech the Chancellor announced a 2% reduction in the basic rate of Income Tax to 25% and a single higher rate of 40%. This major reform will, according to the Chancellor, leave us with one of the simplest systems of Income Tax in the world.

The main personal tax allowances are going up by twice the statutory requirement to compensate for inflation during 1987. The housekeeper, son's or daughter's services, and dependent relative allowances will be abolished from 6 April 1988.

Personal allowances 1988/89

	£
Married man	4,095
Single person	2,605
Wife's earned income relief	2,605
Additional personal allowance	1,490
Age allowance	
— single or widowed person (age 65-79)	3,180
— married couple (age 65-79)	5,035
— single or widowed person (age 80 and over)	3,310
— married couple (age 80 and over)	5,205
— income limit for age allowance	10,600
Widow's bereavement allowance	1,490
Relief for blind person (each)	540

Income Tax rates 1988/89

Rates of tax applying to all income:

Band of taxable income	Rate of tax	Tax on band	Cumulative tax
£	%	£	£
0—19,300	25	4,825	4,825
Over 19,300	40		

The PAYE tables will give effect to these changes on the first pay date after 14 June 1988.

Company cars

The rates of scale benefit for cars provided by an employer for the use of a director or an employee whose earnings, expenses payments and benefits-in-kind amount to more than £8,500 per annum are doubled for 1988/89. The following rates super-cede those previously announced for 1988/89.

	Cars under 4 years old £	Cars 4 years old or more £
Cars with original market value up to £19,250		
Up to 1400cc	1,050	700
1401cc—2000cc	1,400	940
More than 2000cc	2,200	1,450
Cars with original market value over £19,250		
£19,251—£29,000	2,900	1,940
Over £29,000	4,600	3,060

Mortgage interest relief

The overall limit on borrowings for the purchase of the borrower's home up to which the interest is eligible for tax relief is unchanged at £30,000. However, tax relief for interest on loans taken out to finance improvements to the borrower's home will not be allowed on loans taken out on or after 6 April 1988. Existing home improvement loans are unaffected although relief will not be available on replacement loans.

The £30,000 limit on which interest is available for relief will, in future, apply to each property, rather than to each borrower. This means that two or more people, jointly buying a home, will only obtain tax relief on the interest on £30,000 between them. This will apply to new or replacement loans taken out on or after 1 August 1988. Existing loans are unaffected.

At present, tax relief for interest on loans applied for the purchase or improvement of a property used as the only or main residence for a dependent relative or former or separated spouse of the borrower is allowed within the overall limit of £30,000. It is proposed to abolish this relief where a loan is applied for this purpose on or after 6 April 1988. Relief will continue for the life of existing loans which already qualify under the present law.

Donations to charities

Under the Charity Payroll Deduction Scheme, employees of firms which participate in the scheme are entitled to tax relief on donations to charities. The Finance Bill will double the maximum annual limit that an employee can give under these arrangements from £120 to £240.

Personal equity plans

It is proposed to increase for the year to 31 December 1988 and subsequent years:

(1) The overall limit on the amount which may annually be invested from £2,400 to £3,000;
(2) The amount which may be invested in a Unit Trust or Investment Trust from £420 to £540 (or, if greater, 25% of the total investment);
(3) The 'cash investment limit' from £240 to £300.

Compensation for loss of office

The total amount of redundancy and other lump sum payments received on the termination of employment and which are exempt from tax has been increased from £25,000 to £30,000. There will no longer be tax relief on a proportion of the excess payment over this limit. This change will apply to lump sums paid in respect of a termination of employment which occurs on or after 6 April 1988.

Reform of the taxation of maintenance payments

The tax treatment for maintenance arrangements made from 15 March 1988 is to be subject to new rules and simplified.

The tax treatment of payments under existing arrangements will continue under the present rules for 1988/89 except that individuals who are separated or divorced and receiving payments under existing maintenance arrangements will be exempt from tax on the first £1,490. As a transitional measure, the present rules will also apply to Court Orders applied for on or before 15 March 1988 and made by 30 June 1988, maintenance agreements made before 15 March (provided a copy of the agreement is received by the Inspector of Taxes by 30 June) and Court Orders or agreements made on or after Budget Day 1988 which vary or replace such orders or agreements.

For new Court Orders made after Budget Day and maintenance agreements made on or after 15 March 1988, all payments will be made without deduction of tax and the recipient will no longer be liable to tax on the payments received. The payer will be entitled to a form of restricted tax relief up to an amount equal to the difference between the single and married person's allowances.

New Deeds of Covenant
A major change in the tax treatment of non-charitable covenants made by individuals on or after 15 March 1988 has been introduced. The Chancellor has abolished tax relief for payments made by individuals under new Deeds of Covenant while, at the same time, exempting recipients from taxation on the payments received.

The tax treatment for charitable covenants remains unchanged as does that for covenants made by individuals before 15 March 1988 provided they are received by the tax office by the end of June 1988.

Forestry
The tax treatment of commercial woodlands is to be completely reformed and the tax shelter provided by this form of investment is to end.

Independent taxation of husband and wife
In his Budget speech the Chancellor outlined his proposals for a major reform of the tax treatment of married couples which are aimed at removing a number of tax penalties on marriage under the present system. The centrepiece of this reform is a new system of independent taxation for husband and wife which will take effect from 6 April 1990. It will bring with it:
(1) Independent taxation of the incomes of husbands and wives;
(2) Independence and privacy for married women in their tax affairs;
(3) A new structure of Income Tax allowances incorporating a full personal allowance for married women, a new married couples allowance and higher allowances for elderly wives;
(4) Independent taxation of capital gains.

Under independent taxation husbands and wives will each take responsibility for their own tax affairs and for paying the tax due on their own incomes. For the first time married women will become taxpayers in their own right and married men will no longer be responsible for their wives' tax affairs.

Value Added Tax

The limit at which it is necessary to register for VAT is increased to outputs of £22,100 p.a. (previously £21,300 p.a.). The quarterly registration limit is also increased to £7,500 from £7,250.

Application for cancellation of registration for VAT will be possible from 1 June 1988 where predicted future turnover is not expected to exceed £21,100 p.a. exclusive of VAT (previously £20,300).

From 16 March 1988 the fixed penalty for late registration of 30% of the net tax due is revised as follows:

(1) Registration no more than 9 months late		10%
(2) Registration over 9 months but not more than 18 months late		20%
(3) Registration more than 18 months late		30%

There will still be a minimum penalty of £50.

Capital Gains Tax

In an effort to eliminate 'inflationary' gains from the charge to tax, the Chancellor is proposing a radical change in the computation of gains, combined with adjustments to existing exemptions and reliefs, and to the rate of tax payable.

Gains relating to the period prior to 31 March 1982 are to be eliminated by using 31 March 1982 values as the base value in computing gains. The Indexation Allowance will continue to apply. There will be provisions to ensure that the new rules will not produce a bigger gain or loss than would have been the case under the existing regime.

The amount of an individual's gains in the tax year exempt from Capital Gains Tax is reduced from £6,600 to £5,000. For the purposes of the £5,000 exemption the gains made by husband and wife will continue to be aggregated.

The rate of tax payable for 1988/89 onwards will be the rate appropriate to an individual's top slice of income.

It is proposed to abolish the Capital Gains Tax relief for

homes provided free for a dependent relative. This change will apply for disposals on or after 6 April 1988.

Where a disposal of your business assets on retirement takes place after 6 April 1988 further relief of 50% on gains between £125,000 and £500,000 will be allowed.

Losses realised on or after 18 January 1988 from the disposal of shares held in a Personal Equity Plan will not be allowable against other gains for Capital Gains Tax purposes unless the plan is closed before the qualifying period expires.

Inheritance Tax

The Chancellor proposes only one amendment to existing exemptions and reliefs but a substantial simplification and reduction in the rates of tax payable.

At present, gifts totalling in excess of £100,000 to political parties made on death or within the year prior to death are chargeable to tax on the excess over £100,000. That limit is to be abolished and accordingly such gifts will be wholly exempt in the same way as gifts to charities.

The threshold below which no tax is payable has been increased from £90,000 to £110,000. Thereafter a single rate of 40% applies.